JONAH
AND ME

T0155381

JONAH AND ME

ON MISSION WITH GOD

CHUCK DAVIS

BEAUFORT BOOKS

JONAH & ME

Copyright © 2017 by Chuck Davis

All Scripture quotations, unless otherwise noted, are from the ESV: The Holy Bible, English Standard Version, copyright © 2001 by Crossway Bibles, a division of Good News Publishers. Used by permission. All rights reserved.

All rights reserved. No part of this book may be reproduced in any form or by any electronic or mechanical means, including information storage and retrieval systems, without permission in writing from the publisher, except by a reviewer who may quote brief passages in a review.

Library of Congress Cataloging-in-Publication Data on file.

For inquiries about volume orders, please contact:
Beaufort Books
27 West 20th Street, Suite 1102
New York, NY 10011
sales@beaufortbooks.com

Published in the United States by Beaufort Books
www.beaufortbooks.com

Distributed by Midpoint Trade Books
www.midpointtrade.com

Printed in the United States of America

Book Designed by Mark Karis
Cover illustration by Gremlin

CONTENTS

ACKNOWLEDGEMENTS

I AM GRATEFUL FOR MY GODLY HERITAGE. When you write a book with the idea that God is telling a story much larger than your life, you realize that your chapter is not the first.

John and Philena Stebbins and Charles and Beulah Davis, my grandparents, set a clear direction toward Jesus. Both sets of grandparents followed a calling to the vocation of pastor and wife. They gave me a sanctified vision that God might use my life in a calling to the ministry of the Word. These two family lines joined and gave me the spiritual DNA as a preacher and teacher.

And for my parents, Charles and Louise, who gave me a

foundation of security that allowed me to chase a life of faith and risk on mission with God. I would not be who and where I am at today without the solid foundation they established.

I also have the privilege of being on mission with a wife who is fully given to God's calling in her own and our collective life together. On our wedding day, Ingrid Ellen Johannessen declared the following vows before God and the witnesses gathered, "I will go where you go." She has not shrunk back one bit from that promise. In fact, she has gone beyond where I have gone, in the mission that God has shaped for her. She is a servant leader to the global church and mission of God. We are doing this together.

And for my three adult children, Christian, Linnea, and Jordan, who were initially dragged without choice on this family calling to the nations. When I see you live out your calling to be on mission with God, it makes me soar in gratefulness for how you opted in on your own accord. As I look to the future, I pray for my legacy, the generations to come from you who will also choose to partner with God on mission.

I am a blessed man.

MARCH 6, 2017

1

SENT: LIVING ON PURPOSE

I HAVE LIVED THE MOST AMAZING LIFE. I underline the word LIVED! I have not just existed. I have not just gotten by. Life has not just happened to me. I have LIVED!

Now as I say that, I need to be transparent. There have been moments where I succumbed to merely existing. There have been seasons and moments that challenged my sense of purposefulness. But I have always been rescued and restored to my LIVING by my undergirding philosophy that there is a purpose for my life. As a result, I would return to living on purpose.

My life has been given to encourage, train, equip, and exhort people to live on purpose.

I would call this my life's purpose. I heard the question once, "if you had to describe yourself in one word, what would it be?" That is a hard question, as I would like a few more words or the ability to use another language that packs more descriptors into one word than normal English verbs.

But if I were to choose one word I think it would be SENT.

There are a number of questions that immediately come to mind. Sent by whom? Sent where? Sent to do what? Sent how, and with whom? When will I arrive? How will I know?

Sent by whom? God. My purpose is not self-determined or self-created. It is also not narcissistic in a modern sense of self-realization.

Sent where? Before the sending was a calling. God called me back into relationship with himself even when I was bent on running from him. That relationship became the basis of my well founded identity and subsequent sense of the purposefulness for life.

With that foundation of relationship in place, God then sent me out to use my life in fulfilling his primary purpose for me. And I believe that we all have the same underlying primary purpose. He wants us to use our lives to help fellow humans be reconnected to their Creator and to Live on Purpose by joining him in his purpose.

Now for me this has meant following a vocational track that I would define as "the ministry of the Word." In application this has meant that I have been a pastor, missionary, and professor. But Living on Purpose is not only for those who are called to vocational ministry. I learned about Living on Purpose from my father, who was an executive with Bethlehem Steel

Corporation. As a result, I have an underlying desire to call all people, especially those in vocations that are often labeled secular, to Live on Purpose.

This book will continue to answer the follow-up questions surrounding being SENT, toward the goal of calling you to Live on Purpose. If you are Living on Purpose already, my desire is that you would be sharpened in your application of that purpose or simply inspired to keep on.

As I wrestled with my one word answer to the question, *how would you describe yourself?*, another word popped into my mind. STEWARDED. Now that one is obviously going to take some explanation.

Lynn A. Miller is quoted as saying, "Stewardship is all about organizing my life so God can spend me." The very core thought to this statement is that my life is not my own—it is all gift from God. My physical body. My essence, what might be called my inner person. My time. The opportunities afforded me. Right now. I bring all of these resources to God for so that he can spend me in the accomplishment of his purposes.

And since my LIFE is a gift, I own none of it. I am to steward it. Since I am mere manager, God gets first order in determining how my life is to be spent. Thus Living on Purpose must begin with the exercise of figuring out God's larger purpose for my life. As I have already stated— it is the same purpose for all of us. It merely has different places and means for application.

When we begin to organize our lives around his purpose, there is this overwhelming sense of peace and meaningfulness that comes to our lives. It has led my wife and I to embrace the following prayer as a daily exercise in living fully and with a great sense of fulfillment and freedom from anxiety.

Lord, come I this day to you!
I am not a great gift to offer you.
It is my coming that is my gift.
For who among us holds within themselves any worthy offering
*   to the God who owns the universe?*
To come to you while the entire world moves away from
*   you, is our only gift of worth.*
And so I come this day:
ignore me or use me,
save me or spend me.
Use me or set me by, I am yours.
Amen

I want the same for you. I want you to have the privilege of praying this prayer daily— fully alive, fully free, fully fulfilled!

2

YOUR LIFE MATTERS

DAILY WE HEAR—AND SAY—things that betray humankind's sense of a loss of purpose, of design:

Whatever.
Good luck!
That was a crazy coincidence.

And yet, complicated beings that we are, we continue to betray a desire for purpose:

If there is a God, why do so many people suffer?
Why was I born—here and now?
Have I made a difference in at least one life?

These philosophical statements press directly into the question of the purposefulness of life.

Are life and history random, or is there something bigger going on? This is one underlying question that I will address in this book. This question could be posed another way: ***Is God telling a bigger story?*** The answer to this question has personal implications for you and me. If there is a purposeful narrative, we want to know its plot so that we might proactively cooperate with the main storyline: ***How does* my** *story fit with the plot of God's larger story?*

Already, I am exposing some foundational beliefs of my own worldview. I am assuming a creative order. When I look out at the world, observe the patterns of history, hear the stories of people around me, and rehearse the events of my own life, I cannot find a better conclusion than that there is a larger design to our world and our lives. My experiences and observations suggest there are too many coincidences, too many connections of purpose, too many "aha" moments to embrace a perspective of randomness to life. Over the long course of history, I see the working out of principles indicating a larger, purposeful storyline, one that is clearly expressed in the biblical narrative. This storyline is most notably conveyed in the expansion of God's Kingdom around the globe.

In these few paragraphs I am also revealing my assumption that not only is there a personal Creator, but that that Creator remains actively engaged in his world. I do not have enough faith to believe that the amazing order of this world—seen in even in the simple design of the human body and mind—is a result of a random spontaneous combustion or of a non-directed cooperation of raw matter to evolve to a better state. I consider myself a man of faith, but such a leap of faith is beyond my faith capacity. Instead, I embrace a worldview that involves a purposeful Creator and Sustainer behind a purposeful and amazing creation.

My acknowledgement of the Creator and his purposefulness does not mean that I have not questioned the way history and our lives unfold. My view of God, the world, history, and my own existence is laced with mystery. There is much more that I cannot explain than that which I can explain.

And I am daily perplexed and concerned by the observable signs and consequences of the brokenness of so much of creation. Suffering sometimes does feel quite random. I personally have not suffered much in life, but I have friends whose lives seem riddled with suffering. There is no good explanation as to why the discrepancy exists.

The very fact that I have the space and time to reflect philosophically on these questions is a result of my having been born in the right place, at the right time, with the best of life circumstances and the relative ease of life situations, especially with regards to health and provisions. This too might feel random. The men or women in impoverished conditions, who put every bit of energy into merely keeping their children alive through drought, war, and famine, do not have the same luxury.

So why do I have this opportunity and they do not? Certainly it is not because I deserve it more. It is not that I have a higher moral character or greater importance in life. It is not because the purposeful Creator loves me more. Thus, even as I speak about the purposefulness of God's plan, these areas remain totally mysterious to me. I do believe, though, that we can work toward an understanding of the causes of brokenness through looking at the biblical backdrop of fallen creation and spiritual battle. However, knowing this still does not erase all my questions.

In order to answer such questions, some people adopt Deism as their worldview, believing in creative design while at the same time trying to explain the randomness of some suffering and pain. Deism suggests that order is seen in Creation's original design but that God created a closed world system. Suffering, then, is not random, but is the result of certain rules within the creative order, rules God set in place but with which he does not now interfere. This view might be called the *God as Watchmaker* analogy: the world is a finely-tuned system that God initiated—thus the underlying design we observe—but which he then lets run without interference. Somehow, the Fall impacted the working mechanism; the watch was broken and its workings continue to deteriorate over time, but the watchmaker does not open it up for repair. This is a way of explaining the mystery of why an all-loving and all-powerful God does not constantly interrupt the system to ease or end pain and suffering.

I do not find this philosophy satisfying simply because of the reality of miracles. A miracle by definition is an intervention that cannot be explained by natural processes. I have experienced miracles—immediate healings that cannot be explained by medical science, connections that changed lives dramatically, connections that are too purposeful to be explained as randomness; unexplainable shifts in weather and natural order. I cannot muster the intellectual dishonesty to explain those events away, so I am left with a world with which God is engaged and in which he intervenes. But, I am still left with the mystery of when and in what ways he chooses to intervene.

Another theological solution that some have applied to this mystery is what I would call "domineering theism." In an attempt to logically bring all of these conflicting notions together, God is described as sovereign despot. Suffering becomes a tool in his hands. In other words, he is God, so he can do whatever he wants to his creation without needing to explain. I agree with the Otherness of God; he is not obligated to give an accounting to his creation. This aspect of God is evidenced in his response to Job, who questioned God out of his overwhelming personal suffering: "Where were you when I laid the foundations of the world?" (Job 38:4). However, God's response was not an uncaring backhand to Job in support of random and arbitrary use of suffering. God was moving Job to a deeper understanding of and relationship with his god even in the midst of his suffering.

The overall message of Scripture is that God is Sovereign in his love and in his good intention for us. As such, he has a way of redeeming suffering and working good from an apparently evil situation. This is far different than saying that suffering is a tool in his hands, which feels like proactive malice.

So where does that leave us?

Design? Yes.

Randomness? No.

A God who is engaged with his creation? Yes.

A mechanical intervention of a Creator God? No.

The worldview that can resolve these conflicting questions in the pursuit of the purposefulness of history and life is found in the very threads of the biblical narrative. Here are some of its elements:

- A God who creates with order
- A creation that rebels, and in doing so, introduces disorder, along with paradise lost
- A kingdom of darkness that operates in suffering and evil to maintain disorder
- A creation that struggles to cooperate with the original design
- A God who intervenes to rescue the creation
- A people rescued, who are then invited to join God in the Restoration Project
- A final prophetic chapter to the story that guarantees restoration or paradise rediscovered.

When we incorporate this larger story into our framework for living, we are liberated to live fully. In essence, we are invited to experience and retell our own stories in light of God's Story. As a result, we end up discovering that purpose and meaning drip from every page of our story, especially the pages riddled with suffering, disappointment, and seeming randomness. Ultimately, we find ourselves cooperating with God in his Restoration Project to bring healing to the broken parts of creation.

Your life matters! This is not a narcissistic declaration of self-exaltation or self-fulfillment. It is a declaration of truth, allowing you to see your life in the flow of what God is doing and to see his invitation to you to become part of his narrative of restoration and hope.

The key to finding meaning in the stories we are living is to better understand the story he is telling. So here we go…

3

LIFE AS STORY

SO WHAT IS THE UNIFYING STORY?

The first step in reading the Bible for meaning and perspective is to understand the backdrop narrative—the Big Story. All of the smaller, situational, historical, and localized stories only make sense with this backdrop in view. Failure to know the plot of the story will keep us in a state of confusion. The flow of God's Big Story can be summarized in four themes.

- Creation—In the beginning it was good, very good.

- Fall—Shortly thereafter, Creation was broken and paradise was lost.

- Rescue—God intervened to offer a new beginning.

- Restoration—God invites us to join him in regaining the paradise that was lost.

Creation. *"In the beginning God created..."* (Genesis 1:1). We could spend hours on the magnificent elements of our world that point to a Designer. Let me just capture three of these mysteries of beauty and design.

First, consider the Earth itself, with its precise alignment within the universe; it is the perfect distance from the sun so that we do not burn up or freeze to death. Then consider that, although the earth each year travels roughly 600 million miles around the sun and spins at about one thousand miles per hour, gravity keeps us from being blown off this six sextillion tons of spinning mass.

Second, consider the migration of monarch butterflies. Over the span of three generations, monarch butterflies migrate from North America to South America and back, with each generation starting where the previous one left off, continuing the trans-migration across continents without instruction. Something is coded into their DNA, passing beyond their own experience to live within their offspring and their offspring's offspring.

Third, consider the manner in which humans learn language as children. Each society has developed an encoded and incredibly complex system and yet it is learned by two-year-olds.

These are merely three examples from a world that offers millions of inexplicable mysteries. The Bible declares that the wonder and order behind these mysteries is a result of the magnificence of the Designer: *"and it was good, very good"* (Genesis 1:25, 31). The very thought of the magnificence of the Creator behind the amazing creation presses the biblical respondent to praise:

> *"When I look at your heavens, the work of your fingers . . .*
> *O Lord, our Lord, how majestic is your name in all the earth!"*
>   (Psalm 8:3, 9).

> *"I praise you for I am fearfully and wonderfully made. Wonderful*
> *are your works; my soul knows it very well"* (Psalm 139:14).

The Fall. While Genesis 1 and 2 provide a theological explanation for the beauty and complexity of the world that we live in, Genesis 3 blaringly interrupts that beautiful song. Paradise becomes marred, at least for a period of time. The beautifully cultivated ecosystem of God's garden is taken over by weeds and now demands human toil to maintain it. The divine commission to humans to exercise authority to co-create with God in the keeping of the garden is forfeited to another ruler. The results are a misuse of power and the entrance of broken relationships: with God, with each other, and even with ourselves. The way of blessing becomes a way that involves curse. The *good* and the *very good* become marred. In addition, suffering now enters the world as a result of our rebellion from God's original design.

In the same way that I could devote hours to the beauty and magnificence of creation, I could spend hours recounting the overwhelming results of brokenness that point to this evil presence in the world. The evil is so unimaginable that it cannot be simply explained by the notion of society's failure to educate children about how to live; one must accept the notion of original sin. Evil is insidious, as a few examples will show.

First, there are fathers who are so lost that, when they are unable to provide for their family, they resort to selling their daughters, even while knowing those daughters will become sex slaves. Worse yet, there are men who abuse their own family members to satisfy their own broken sexuality.

Secondly, national strife, wars, and rumors of wars point to the brokenness of humanity. Jesus predicted that such a hostile environment would be present in the latter days (Matthew 24:4-6).

We see a third example of the brokenness of humanity in those who have lost a sense of the value of human life. On the one hand, there is the lonely man, so ostracized that he believes the only way for him to feel again is to take the lives of innocent children, ones who have no connection to his own pain. On the other hand, there is the young woman who decides that ending her own life prematurely is better than working through the numbness caused by a loss of purpose.

The Bible declares that the comprehensiveness and repulsiveness of evil cannot be assigned to God. Instead, the blame rests with Satan, a rebellious spirit-being, strong, but not equal to God, one who works in purposeful opposition to God's creative work of goodness, life, and beauty. This rebellious spirit is Satan, the devil, the enemy of our souls. He leads a kingdom of rebels, a kingdom given foothold at the Fall, when humans first rebelled against God. Satan maintains disorder and inflicts harm through broken worldly systems and through the cooperation of us humans in our fallen fleshly state. God is not responsible for pain and suffering; this is the work of the kingdom of darkness. The dark kingdom both uses pain and entices us into situations where we create our own pain. This reality is expressed clearly in the descriptions of its leader:

"the accuser" (Revelation 12:10; Zechariah. 3:1)

"the deceiver" (Revelation 20:10)

"blinder to spiritual light" (I Corinthians 4:4)

"the dragon" (Revelation 12:7)

"a murderer and a liar" (John 8:44)

"the destroyer" (Rev. 9:11)

"the tempter" (Matt. 4:3)

"the evil one" (Matt. 13:38)

Rescue. The next portion of the biblical story after the Fall, describes the process of God preparing and executing a rescue. He observes that humans are bent on being their own gods, so the peoples become divided—within and without, separated from one another through language and geography (Genesis 11).

At Creation God began with a family; in the rescue he begins again with a new family (Genesis 12). He chooses

Abraham to be this new family's earthly father of faith. Abraham is not perfect; the blemish of the fall is observable in his own attitudes and actions. But in spite of Abraham's broken faith, God establishes a covenant with this new family, the family that will be his solution for rescue and restoration.

This family becomes a nation that is called to help rescue other nations by inviting them into a restored relationship with God (Exodus 19). This family/nation is to serve as mediator between God and the scattered people. But the stain of sin, seen in their rejection of God's way, is too much to overcome: the new family struggles to share with others the blessing of restored relationship with the Creator God.

God, though, will not let the sins of humans stop him in his loving pursuit. We were created in love and, even though we rebelled against this loving God, he continues to pursue us in love. Eventually, out of this chosen family comes a Son, who will give love fully back to us. This is Jesus, and he is unique, unlike any of the other human sons. As one born of woman and adopted by man, he is representative of the original Adam. But his true origin is of God, begotten of God by the Holy Spirit. The other sons are made of clay and are shaped by the Potter's hands, but this new Son is the Potter himself—Creator and created in one. As one with divine origin, Jesus lives in perfection, inwardly untouched by sin; and from the beginning, though he was tempted just as other humans are, he resisted the outward temptation to sin (Matthew 4; Hebrews 4:15).

God sent this Jesus to rescue the human family, to buy it back from the slavery into which it had sold itself. Whereas the Fall introduced slavery, the Son introduces freedom, freedom for us to live out God's purpose. God does not buy back his creation as a commodity to be used. Rather, God's love is a pursuing love (Luke 15). He pursues us beyond our rebellion in order to buy us back so that he might adopt us back into the God family. God loves outlandishly, showing the depths of his love in the purchase price: the death of his one and only Son.

Theologically, this act of purchasing us out of slavery is called redemption. From a human perspective, it might be called a second chance. Through his death on the cross, the Son paid in blood for our sins, thus buying us back out of slavery and allowing us to rejoin God's family. All who choose to allow him to stand on the slave block in their place are rescued, restored to the family and given this second chance.

Our stories of second chances are called testimonies. People regularly give witness to the life transformation that comes through Jesus as a result of this rescue. Although it would take hours to tell even the few stories that I have heard, I will briefly mention three that mean much to me.

First is the rescue of my grandfather. He did not have a good childhood. He experienced abuse and rejection from his own family. But on February 10, 1929, in a small Methodist church, he heard good news—there is liberation for the abused and rejected. That day, the blinders on his heart were removed, and he came running into the arms of a Prodigal God. With his rescue, my family line was re-entwined with the God story in spectacular ways, and my own life was changed forever.

Second is the story of my own rescue: August 3, 1969. Not everyone can name the day and time when they were rescued. Some of us walk slowly into the Kingdom of God without noticeable event or fanfare. It could be said that I had already been walking toward the Kingdom, but the moment I entered in is clear in my mind. As a nine-year-old boy, I was invited by my grandmother to quit standing outside the rescue and to receive the invitation of the Prodigal God to come fully home. I was overwhelmed with my sinful nature. What could a nine-year-old boy have done to feel such conviction of culpability? How could my heart be so clearly aware of my own rebellion? And how does a simple prayer accepting a Rescuer change weeping of despair into tears of joy? These are profound and mysterious questions requiring profound answers. Suffice it to say: I was rescued. My story was changed forever and made more full in the present season of forever..

Third is the rescue of my own children, both biological and spiritual. My three now-adult children each had a moment when they allowed Jesus to stand on the slave block in their place, and I have watched them each walk into the reality of that faith in their own ways. Through my ministry, I have also had the privilege of inviting dozens into renewed relationship with the Prodigal God. As each responded, they were adopted back into the God family through Jesus Christ. Their stories were re-entwined with the God story in spectacular ways. And their lives were changed forever.

> *But God, being rich in mercy, because of the great love with which he loved us, even when we were dead in our trespasses, made us alive together with Christ—by grace you have been saved... For by grace you have been saved through faith. And this is not your own doing; it is the gift of God, not a result of works, so that no one may boast. For we are his workmanship, created in Christ Jesus for good works, which God prepared beforehand, that we should walk in them* (Ephesians 2:4-5, 8-10).

Therefore, if anyone is in Christ, he is a new creation. The old has passed away; behold, the new has come (II Corinthians 5:17).

But to all who did receive him, who believed in his name, he gave the right to become children of God (John 1:12).

See what kind of love the Father has given to us, that we should be called children of God; and so we are (I John 3:1).

Restoration. The human family is not only saved from the stain and penalty of sin; it is saved to purposefulness in partnering with God in his Restoration Project. After his death for us on the cross, the God-man, Jesus, ascended into heaven to take the positional place of authority in the throne room of God. From there he directs and empowers this Restoration Project, and he promises to return one day to finalize the recovery. From there, he also invites God's adopted family to find their purpose by joining in the rescue of others.

That rescue of others is a war. The cross and resurrection declare freedom, but freedom must often be won through continuous battles. In this case, the war is between God's Kingdom, where we serve as adopted children; and Satan's Kingdom, where humans serve as slaves. The war is already won. The continuous battles, the ongoing skirmishes, are the ratification of that victory being played out in each generation and in each person's life. God's adopted sons and daughters are called to be conquerors in these battles that are taking place in between Christ's first coming and his return. This call of God is actually a renewed version of the original call, a call we forfeited at the Fall. It is a call to walk with delegated authority and to return to God what rightfully belongs to him: creation—both people and land.

The Creator's greatest delight is when people are restored to him in vibrant relationship. Thus the call is to bring people into such a relationship, inviting them to leave the kingdom of darkness and return to the kingdom of light. The Creator's delight gets expressed fully when his Kingdom overtakes the kingdoms of this world—which means full recovery in personhood (salvation, healing of body and soul, deliverance), in society (right relationships), in culture (renewed vocation and justice), and on the earth (stewardship of the land). God's desire to restore his relationship with people and his desire to have his adopted sons and daughters participate in this restoration is seen throughout the Bible.

> *"Peace be with you. As the Father has sent me, even so I am sending you"* (John 20:21).

> *"But you will receive power when the Holy Spirit has come upon you, and you will be my witnesses in Jerusalem and in all Judea and Samaria, and to the end of the earth"* (Acts 1:8).

> *"Therefore, we are ambassadors for Christ, God making his appeal through us. We implore you on behalf of Christ, be reconciled to God"* (II Corinthians 5:20).

Every human being is touched by the first two large themes of the big story: Creation and Fall. All are created precious by God. All are born with purpose. All are image bearers of God. However, at the same time, all are marred by the Fall. We all participate in the human folly of rebelling against God's way. This rebellion is part of our inheritance of sin, but we also willingly opt into the fallen condition. The impact of the Fall manifests itself differently in each of us, but the one element that is true for all of us is the need for a rescue.

This is where the good news, the gospel, comes in. Jesus has provided Rescue for everyone who will receive salvation from him. He reaches out to each of us with arms outstretched on a cross. He does not force us to respond, as that would be contrary to love. Because of this, not all will become part of God's chapter on rescue; instead some choose not to be rescued.

C.S. Lewis once said, "There are only two kinds of people in the end: those who say to God, 'Thy will be done,' and those to whom God says, in the end, 'Thy will be done.'"[1] A significant motivation for the people of God to be on mission is so that every person has the chance to make that willful decision based on a full understanding of God's love.

This good news goes beyond rescue to a restoration of purpose. God invites us, and in fact, exhorts us, to be part of his Restoration Project. Once we ourselves have been rescued, we are immediately deputized into his Restoration Project. We become the bearers of his Kingdom benefits and transformation. Not all of the rescued, though, naturally enter into this renewed sense of purpose. We get distracted with everyday life. We join faith communities that can become insular and not outreaching. We find ourselves in societies that have not only begun telling a different narrative story, they have become antagonistic to this story that God is telling.

The story of Jonah is perfect to model this recovery and call into the Restoration Project for multiple reasons. Jonah is a living metaphor for all the restored people of God. Once a person is rescued from danger, the temptation is to play it safe. Jonah, like so many of us, wanted to play it safe. In addition, Jonah is a good example because his personal story is a localized example of the four themes or stages of the Big Story. He graphically illustrates the challenge embedded in all of our stories. Will we be rescued? Once we are rescued, will we join the Restoration Project? Rescue reestablishes our identity—God makes a name for us. Restoration reignites our purpose for living—we become ambassadors of a better Kingdom.

PART I

JONAH: A LIVING METAPHOR

THE ELEPHANT IN THE ROOM—so was it really a big fish?
We could easily get sidetracked on this opening question.
I am going to disappointment many people with my answer.
I don't think it really matters. I do not think the integrity of
God's Word is on the line based on whether or not there was
an actual man named Jonah and an actual big fish. The story of
Jonah could be an allegory that was crafted to point to a bigger
problem—the unwillingness of God's people to step out of our
comfort zone to be involved in his Restoration Project.

Personally, I have no problem believing that God could

miraculously use a storm and a big fish in the life of a prophet-missionary. I have experienced situations and events in my life that can only be explained with the word "miracle". As mentioned earlier, I do not subscribe to a closed universe—God the watchmaker never opening up the back of the watch to make corrections. Doing so would mean that my faith would not have space for a literal resurrection. Honestly, my whole faith is rooted in the bodily resurrection of the crucified Jesus. The historical evidence is too great to believe otherwise; thus, I would have to suspend my own reason and faith experience to deny the possibility of God entering into the creative order to do things in an abnormal way.

All of that is to say that I believe that God could have kept a man alive in the belly of a great fish to accomplish a greater purpose. Thus, out of my tradition and experience, I believe there was an actual guy named Jonah, who chartered passage in a boat headed toward Tarshish, who got thrown overboard, who was saved by God through the intervention of a large fish, and who got a second chance to live out his calling to bring rescue and the Restoration Project to Ninevah. In his Word, God has chosen to preserve the real life story of a man named Jonah to challenge each of us in our own stories. Will we, the rescued, allow our hearts to be transformed enough to join our Creator in his Restoration Project? Jonah is a local and contextual story, retelling the Big Story into our stories to invite us to engage purposefully in the Big Story.

Now, noting my beliefs on this story, I have no problem with people who see the tale as a finely crafted short story designed to make a point. To me that does not make it any less true! The story, whether literal or crafted as a theological metaphor, is still true—it shines light on God's challenge to the condition of our heart. So many people are so worried about defending the integrity of the text as literal that they end up missing the whole point. The Bible is both history and literature—it is a theological story and historical recounting. And all the time, it is telling a bigger story, one well beyond the literal and locality of each account. And it is true!

Scot McKnight captures this reality so well in a passing phrase in his book *The Blue Parakeet:*

> Missing the difference between God and the Bible is a bit like the person who reads Jonah and spends hours and hours to figure out if a human can live inside of a whale—and what kind of whale it was—but never encounters God. The book is about Jonah's God, not Jonah's whale.[1]

So, given the possibility of both ways of reading the story— literally with a deeply embedded metaphorical message or metaphorically as a theological exhortation to the people of God—I invite you into a local rendition of the Big Story. I will be reading it literally from this point on. You can approach the text in the way you feel most appropriate. In the end, we must all read it theologically, which is as a call to a transformation of heart and to engaging action.

4

JONAH: A MAN ON THE RUN

CREATION AND THE FALL

1 Now the word of the LORD came to Jonah the son of Amittai, saying, ² "Arise, go to Nineveh, that great city, and call out against it, for their evil has come up before me." ³ But Jonah rose to flee to Tarshish from the presence of the LORD. He went down to Joppa and found a ship going to Tarshish. So he paid the fare and went down into it, to go with them to Tarshish, away from the presence of the LORD.

⁴ But the LORD *hurled a great wind upon the sea, and there was a mighty tempest on the sea, so that the ship threatened to break up. ⁵ Then the mariners were afraid, and each cried out to his god. And they hurled the cargo that was in the ship into the sea to lighten it for them. But Jonah had gone down into the inner part of the ship and had lain down and was fast asleep. ⁶ So the captain came and said to him, "What do you mean, you sleeper? Arise, call out to your god! Perhaps the god will give a thought to us, that we may not perish."*
⁷ And they said to one another, "Come, let us cast lots, that we may know on whose account this evil has come upon us." So they cast lots, and the lot fell on Jonah. ⁸ Then they said to him, "Tell us on whose account this evil has come upon us. What is your occupation? And where do you come from? What is your country? And of what people are you?" ⁹ And he said to them, "I am a Hebrew, and I fear the LORD, *the God of heaven, who made the sea and the dry land." ¹⁰ Then the men were exceedingly afraid and said to him, "What is this that you have done!" For the men knew that he was fleeing from the presence of the* LORD, *because he had told them.*
¹¹ Then they said to him, "What shall we do to you, that the sea may quiet down for us?" For the sea grew more and more tempestuous. ¹² He said to them, "Pick me up and hurl me into the sea; then the sea will quiet down for you, for I know it is because of me that this great tempest has come upon you." ¹³ Nevertheless, the men rowed hard to get back to dry land, but they could not, for the sea grew more and more tempestuous against them. ¹⁴ Therefore they called out to the LORD, *"O* LORD, *let us not perish for this man's life, and lay not on us innocent blood, for you, O* LORD, *have done as*

it pleased you." ¹⁵ So they picked up Jonah and hurled him into the sea, and the sea ceased from its raging. ¹⁶ Then the men feared the LORD exceedingly, and they offered a sacrifice to the LORD and made vows.

¹⁷ And the LORD appointed a great fish to swallow up Jonah. And Jonah was in the belly of the fish three days and three nights.

Shawna was a typical four-year-old, strong-willed girl. She had her own plans and ideas, ones that didn't always match her parents' plans. She would often take off on her tricycle, unconcerned about how far she wandered from home. Her mom, trying to set up boundaries, one day said, "Now, Shawna, you can ride your tricycle on the driveway and up the sidewalk to that tree, but you can't go past that tree. This is for your safety. If you go beyond that spot I am going to have to give you a spanking. Now I am going inside; I have a few things to do. When I come out, I want to find you in this spot." Shawna thought about it for a moment, then pointed toward the forbidden zone and said, "Mom, you might as well give me a spanking now. I've got places to go."

In Jonah, we read the story of a man who also had places to go. He wrestles, though, with going where God wants to send him, and even when he finally does go, he is not sure he wants to be there. This man's life stands as an illustration of God's Big Story: of creation, fall, rescue, and restoration in the eventual alignment of our lives with God to be in that place where he can use us most fruitfully.

Jonah captures our interest initially because, unlike most of the Old Testament prophets, whose messages are delivered primarily[1] in words, Jonah delivers a message of exhortation through his very actions. The book of Jonah is a narrative of what a prophet does and doesn't do in response to God's call. We can call Jonah the "incarnational prophet" as he wrestles with God's design and plan. His very life story embodies the struggle of a people called by God to be used in the Restoration Project.

INTERPRETATION OF JONAH 1

We begin the story of Jonah in chapter 1, verse 1, with a call:

Now the word of the Lord came to Jonah the son of Amittai.

"The word of the Lord came." This phrase occurs more than one hundred times in the Hebrew Scriptures. It signals that God is calling someone, or a group of people, to a unique role in his Restoration Project. We can be skimming along in Scriptures when suddenly God inserts himself more prominently in the story: "The word of the Lord came." We are aware that God is behind the scenes all the time, but our attention is grabbed in these moments. **God is always present; he is just not always obvious.** Eugene Petersen has stated that the most fundamental truth is not that God is, but that God communicates, and in these words to Jonah we are witness to that direct communication.

It would be nice to know what was going on in Jonah's life at the time God's word came to him. Was he actively following God? Was he used to hearing from God, or was this something new? Did he have something else going on that would need to be set aside? Family? Work? Aspirations? Was he a prophet before the divine intervention, or is this the beginning of his prophetic ministry? Knowing these details could help us to discern when God is speaking to us. We don't know these details, though. However, we do know that Jonah was called by God. So, let's dive a bit deeper into the text for nuances of that calling.

The speaker of this calling is God. The Hebrew language uses a variety of names for God, each name focusing on a particular aspect of God's character and each name evoking a different response in the Hebrew hearers of the story. The Hebrew word used here for God is translated *the* LORD. In many English translations of the Bible, the use of uppercase letters (LORD) or lowercase letters (Lord) gives a clue to which name of God is being used in Hebrew. *LORD* is our English translation of the Hebrew word Yahweh (הָוֹהְי), or Jehovah. This was a special name that God revealed through Moses to his people, his new family (Exodus 3:14). There were other names for God, for example, those describing him as Creator and Sustainer of the universe; but Yahweh was the intimate name of God, the name that he revealed uniquely to his chosen people. In this first verse of Jonah, God isn't named as Elohim (מִיהֹלֱא), the God of the nations. The God who speaks to Jonah is Yahweh, the intimate revelation of God to the Jews.

The one receiving this call is Jonah. His name literally means "dove," which is the symbol of peace. He is further identified as the son of Amittai, which means "the son of faithfulness." Immediately we are face-to-face with a dilemma: will the etymology of Jonah's name match his conduct? Names in the Bible are not simply tags to identify a particular person; they signify things such as character, history, or divine purpose. We quickly see, however, that Jonah's story is not about peace and faithfulness. He responds in ways opposite to the etymology of his own name. This dove will wrestle with God, and will ultimately be disobedient to God's call. In doing so, he will end up disturbing the peace of those intersecting with his own story. In Jonah's given names we see that he was created for a divine purpose; in the remainder of his story, we will see whether he will accept that purpose or rebel and attempt to create his own purpose. Will he embrace God's call to join His Restoration Project?

Jonah's calling from God is a call to action (verse 2):

> *"Arise, go to Nineveh, that great city, and call out against it, for their evil has come up before me."*

In the original Hebrew, the first words are *"Get up and go."* These words will prove very important in the unfolding of the Jonah story. Jonah, get up and go to Nineveh! The story of Jonah's life is marked by upward and downward trajectory.

Nineveh was the capital of Assyria, five hundred miles to the east of where Jonah lived by land. Assyria was one of the most ruthless empires of that day and one of the nemeses of Israel. The Assyrians extorted taxes from the Israelites and were a constant threat to them and, at different periods of history, they even took the Israelites into captivity. They were the antithesis of the people of God—or at least of what the people of God were supposed to be. Their name was synonymous with cruelty, brutality, and constant danger. History remembers them as a ruthless and sadistic culture.

It is to these people that God sent Jonah. He told Jonah to go to them and address their wickedness. Now that is quite a calling. Jonah was to call the Ninevites to account, showing them that their way was not God's way. Cursing your enemies from a distance of 500 miles is one thing; going to them to confront their wickedness is quite another. While this message was an invitation for Nineveh to find a better way, there was a good chance that they would not receive it well, for it began with a direct challenge: it was time for them to turn from wickedness and darkness and from their own version of the story, a version that did not include God.

Good news in the Bible usually begins with bad news. The bad news, for the Ninevites and for us, is that we are all lost when we live in rebellion to God's prescribed way. Yet the bad news is necessary; we are not going to choose to be rescued if we do not have a sense of being lost, of having fallen. The Ninevites tried to overcome their deviation from course by using aggression and conquest to take charge of their own journey. They may have felt that this was leading them to a better life, but in reality, it was a path leading to destruction.

We get into similar patterns when we use more sophisticated forms of conquest—accumulation, adventure, acting out, attention seeking, to name just a few. We think these are going to restore to us a sense of the good life, just as the Ninevites felt their aggression would bring them the life they wanted. We find out, though, that these pursuits leave us more in want than before. This is the bad news: we are lost in our own ways. The good news is that we can be found in God's way.

We can enter Jonah's story more deeply by identifying with the emotions Jonah must have felt when he heard God's call. Who or what is our Ninevah? Who or what is my greatest "nemesis" today, my greatest enemy? Or whom do I hold at an arm's length because of past things they have done to my people or to me? God invites each of us to face our "enemy." In doing so, we may feel like we need to call the enemy out, to "call out against it." However, we are going to discover through the life journey of the prophet Jonah that this "calling out" must be viewed through the veil of God's love and compassion.

Recognizing our enemies is not so that we can plan how to get back at them. Someone once told me of a great line that they had read in a novel—*good guys don't win when bad guys lose; good guys win when bad guys become good guys.* Rather than cursing our enemies we are to bless them. The greatest blessing is an offer of the good news of God's invitation back into relationship. This will take a radical transformation of our natural way of thinking and feeling. We will see that the reluctant prophet Jonah was not quite ready for that response directed toward his enemies.

After receiving the call from God, Jonah does something that we do not expect from a prophet who has just heard from the LORD (verse 3):

> But Jonah rose to flee to Tarshish from the presence of the LORD.
> He went down to Joppa and found a ship going to Tarshish.
> So he paid the fare and went down into it, to go with them
> to Tarshish, away from the presence of the LORD.

Tarshish, located in Spain, was in the opposite direction from Nineveh. Jonah's rebellious response, though, is evidenced not only in the direction he flees, but also in his willingness to take to the sea. "The waters" for the Hebrew people were the place of chaos. Other peoples lived on the sea, but not the Israelites; land was their environment. Water was associated with danger. Jonah could have traveled over land to fulfill his mission; instead, he chose chaos.

The Scripture is quite clear about his reason for running in the opposite direction: it was "to flee from the Lord." Jonah seems to have been thinking, *If I can get far enough away from this place, maybe God will forget me and I won't have to do anything about his calling.* The absurdity of this thought is exposed in Psalm 139:

> *"You know where I sit, you know when I rise, you perceive my thoughts from afar, you know my going out and all my ways. Where can I go from your spirit? Where can I go from your presence?"*

As a prophet, Jonah should have known the truth of this psalm, that no matter where he went, God would be there with him. The immensity of his desire to get away from his calling must have driven that knowledge from his mind. He knew the truth about God, but he rebelled anyway, reminding us that rebellion is a common trait of even the rescued. We can easily block God's Word out of our conscience when it makes us uncomfortable or doesn't validate a chosen personal preference.

The imagery in the Hebrew text is rich at this point. It says, *"He went down to Joppa."* Remember the call: *"get up and go"*? That is a message many people have heard from God. Abram, for example, heard the message "get up and go." Abram did not even get a destination city in his calling. The LORD told him that the destination would be made clear at a later time. Even with the destination not completely clear, Abram got up and went. The result was blessing—blessings for him and blessings for the nations. We are living out of some of those blessings today. Jonah also received the call to get up and go, but his response led him on successive stages of *going down*.

To go to Joppa from Israel meant that Jonah had to literally *go down*, leaving the plain and descending to sea level. But his descent did not stop there. Once he arrived at the city of Joppa, he *went down* into the ship. Once he was in the ship, he *went down* into the belly of the ship. In the belly of ship, he *lay down* to sleep. After the ship set sail, he was *tossed down* into sea, where he *went down* into the belly of a big fish. Jonah kept going down, down, down. The Hebrew audience would have picked up on the contrary path that Jonah was taking: he traded getting up and going for fleeing and going down.

Without knowing the whole story, we might think at this point that Jonah had now gotten away from the threat or danger of God's call in his life. But if we read on, we will see the story turn into an action adventure.

> But the LORD *hurled a great wind upon the sea, and there was a mighty tempest on the sea, so that the ship threatened to break up* (verse 4).

A storm is a picture of adversity. We discover in this story that adversity oftentimes is God's gift to us, although we may not think so mid-storm. The storm in Jonah's story was violent. The sailors' fear is unmistakable, even though experienced seafarers are used to ships keeling on their sides and launching over waves as they sail into the face of a tempest. Fear is often a result of not knowing, and these sailors had enough experience on the sea to be less driven to fear in this situation than a land dweller like Jonah. But this storm was so ferocious that even these sailors panicked. They began jettisoning all of the cargo—the same cargo that was their livelihood (verse 5a).

Jonah, however, was not afraid; in fact, he was oblivious to what was going on.

But Jonah had gone down into the inner part of the ship and had lain down and was fast asleep (verse 5b).

We humans find many ways to numb ourselves when we are out of touch with our divine calling. Jonah slept. He chose avoidance rather than engagement. The choice of words in the Hebrew text offers an interesting twist. The Hebrew word for deep sleep, *radam* (רָדַם), and the word for descend, *yarad* (דָרַי), are near homonyms. This similarity in sound is hard to pick up at first glance, but the connection is found in the root of each word: -rad. (ya-rad-am). The Hebrew ear would have been tuned to these types of literary devices. Deep sleep was the final place of escape for Jonah as he went down, down, down.

The captain realized the absurdity of sleeping at such a precarious time. He said to Jonah, "How can you sleep? It is time to get up and call unto your god; maybe he will take notice of us and we will not perish." This is an unexpected shift in the story. The pagan captain and the sailors, though unconnected to the one true God, the LORD, acted in a more devout manner than the prophet.

The captain was the antithesis of the prayer-less, careless prophet: "Everyone else is praying; why are you not praying?"

The sailors, using the spiritual rituals familiar to them, cast lots seeking a divine intervention. In their worldview, there was a force at work beyond their own determination to weather the tempest. Although these men were not connected to Yahweh, that did not mean that they did not see a Greater Mover (or Movers in their polytheistic worldview) behind the activities of their world. For the ancients, *atheism* was not a category of thought; all peoples looked for divine engagement in everyday activities. In their worldview, trouble usually meant that it was time to find out what the gods were trying to say.

It was not a perfect science to know the minds of the gods, but this time casting lots worked out perfectly: "and the lot fell on Jonah." Jonah was found to be the reason for the storm, but the sailors had no idea who he was.

Verse 8:

> "Tell us on whose account this evil has come upon us. What is
> your occupation?
> And where do you come from? What is your country? And of
> what people are you?"

Remember this is a story about a prophet. Prophets speak. But in this case, the story goes on for nine verses before we hear the prophet speak. And he doesn't speak until pagan sailors prompt him to. He answers in verse 9:

> "I am a Hebrew, and I fear the LORD, the God of heaven, who
> made the sea and the dry land."

As we see here and throughout this story, the impact of the prophet's message is not due to the quality of the delivery but is due to the One who speaks behind or through the prophet. The prophet's words land with power even though he is not living out of the flow of God's power. People respond to the message of God and actually respond with life changes when given a fresh revelation of the true God.

Jonah then confessed to the men that he was fleeing from the presence of the LORD. The immediate impact of the message is seen in the response of the sailors. *They became terrified.* The storm revealed an angry deity.

There is escalating drama in the story. What would the sailors do with the fleeing prophet, the reason for God's anger? The storm, Jonah, and the God of the fleeing prophet are closely connected. *"What are we going to do with you? What is going to be the solution to this? We worship the gods of the seas and now the sea is trying to destroy us. You proclaim the God of sea and land and say he is responsible for this storm. How are we to respond to his anger?"*

While they are deliberating (verse 11), the LORD added drama to the story by turning the seas more tempestuous. Finally, Jonah takes responsibility, verse 12:

> *"Pick me up and hurl me into the sea; then the sea will quiet down for you, for I know it is because of me that this great tempest has come upon you."*

Once again the sailors show more character than the prophet of God. Instead of throwing him overboard to assure their own safety, they did their best to row back to land. The contrast between their actions and Jonah's is glaring. Here is Jonah, a man of God who had no compassion for a city needing to know the love of God. Here is Jonah, who didn't care about his companions as he sleeps in denial in the belly of the ship. And then, here are the sailors, who would not sacrifice the prophet even though they were being afflicted because of his disobedience.

They attempted to row back to shore. The pagans acted more like God than the prophet did.

> *Nevertheless, the men rowed hard to get back to dry land, but they could not, for the sea grew more and more tempestuous against them* (verse 13).

Then for a third time we are shown the contrast between the right actions of the pagan sailors and the wrong actions of the prophet. In verse 14, we see the sailors invoke the Lord before the prophet does:

> *"O LORD, let us not perish for this man's life, and lay not on us innocent blood, for you, O LORD, have done as it pleased you."*

Lest we forget, God is writing this story, not the prophet or the sailors. Even good intentions and right causes from a human perspective cannot alter God's plan. As the sailors try to do the right thing, God increases the intensity of the storm to deter them because only he sees the bigger picture, and is telling the fuller plot of the story

At the end of their rope and their ability to fight the sea, the sailors finally concluded that Jonah's solution might be the only response they can give to an angry God. So they threw Jonah into the sea, which immediately ceased raging. The clear connection between their action and the calm seas led the men to acknowledge the Lord with sacrifice and to make vows to him.

We come to the famous conclusion of this scene of action and conflict (verse 17):

And the LORD appointed a great fish to swallow up Jonah. And Jonah was in the belly of the fish three days and three nights.

I will talk more about the fish in the next chapter. Here I simply want to highlight what we have already seen in the story. God creates and gives identity and purpose, but a prophet rebels from that original design. He falls. He is in downward spiral. His falling puts others in danger. But God is telling a better story than the one the rebellious prophet is living. The trial that Jonah faces in the chaos of the seas is not only the beginning of his re-rescue; it is a prologue to the rescue of another people. Storms and fish bellies reveal that God's primary goal for us is not comfort but purpose. And the Jonah narrative points out clearly the opposing responses of pagan sailor and called prophet.

The question remains for each of the rescued—will we choose to cooperate with the Divine story or be involuntary players? Life purpose and meaning is magnified when we voluntarily get up and go with God.

5

JONAH: A MAN TURNED AROUND

RESCUE

1 Then Jonah prayed to the LORD his God from the belly of the fish, ² saying,

"I called out to the LORD, out of my distress,
and he answered me;
out of the belly of Sheol I cried,
and you heard my voice

³ *For you cast me into the deep,*
into the heart of the seas,
and the flood surrounded me;
all your waves and your billows
passed over me.

⁴ *Then I said, 'I am driven away*
from your sight;
yet I shall again look
upon your holy temple.'

⁵ *The waters closed in over me to take my life;*
the deep surrounded me;
weeds were wrapped about my head

⁶ *at the roots of the mountains.*
I went down to the land
whose bars closed upon me forever;
yet you brought up my life from the pit,
O LORD my God.

⁷ *When my life was fainting away,*
I remembered the LORD,
and my prayer rose to you,
into your holy temple.

⁸ *Those who pay regard to vain idols*
forsake their hope of steadfast love.

⁹ But I with the voice of thanksgiving
will sacrifice to you;
what I have vowed I will pay.
Salvation belongs to the LORD!"

¹⁰ And the LORD spoke to the fish, and it vomited Jonah out
upon the dry land.

The second chapter of Jonah is a prayer. Jonah finds himself in trouble and he turns back to God. Often we are like Jonah: we remember to pray only when we are in trouble. In those moments, we are often troubled by the simplicity of our prayers. They seem to be solely an SOS beacon. The simplicity of these prayers, though, exhibits raw faith. Sometimes we are embarrassed because when life is going well we seem to drift from a sense of needing to communicate with God. God is not put off by this as much as we might think. All one has to do is remember the parable of the Prodigal God to know how God feels when his troubled sons and daughters come home.

The same profoundness of simple prayers can be seen in the flow of everyday activities. Some of our best prayers are offered up when we are just driving down the road and we think of someone and shoot off a quick intercession up to heaven. Or they take place in the middle of the night: we wake up from a dream in which we sensed a friend or family member in need, and we stand in the gap through prayer. In reality, all of life can become a conversation of prayer with God because God is only a prayer away. This realization means the most when we are in trouble and need rescue.

Jonah was in trouble, and he definitely needed rescue. He

had heard a calling from God that was quite specific; God had asked Jonah to join Him in his Restoration Project. But instead of joining God, Jonah ran. It took just one prayer, though, to get him back on course. We are going to look at Jonah's prayer to see how God rescues us and how repentant prayer aligns our stories to the larger Story that God is telling.

INTERPRETATION OF JONAH 2

Verse 17 of chapter 1 finishes with a description of the problem facing the prophet:

> *And the Lord appointed a great fish to swallow up Jonah. And Jonah was in the belly of the fish three days and three nights.*

Verse 1 of chapter 2 picks up the story right there:

> *Then Jonah prayed to the LORD his God from the belly of the fish.*

Could this really have happened? Is it even possible? What does the text actually say?

The author of this Jonah story likes the word *great* (using it seven times in this short book). God calls Jonah to a *great* city; a *great* wind and tempest arrest Jonah; and a *great* fish returns him. We don't know what kind of fish it was. We have traditionally referred to it as a whale, but the Hebrew text uses the generic word for fish (הַגָּדוֹל).

If the great fish was a whale, it was probably a sperm whale because those are the species that most regularly frequent the Mediterranean Sea. The average bull male is fifty-five feet long (nine people laid out head to toe, or five average-length cars bumper to bumper). Its stomach then would clearly be large enough to hold a wayward prophet. So that part of the story seems plausible, even to those who seek a naturalized explanation. It would still take a miracle of divine intervention, though, to keep the prophet alive while swimming in the digestive juices of the large fish. The problem is that miracles *aren't* plausible; if they were, they wouldn't be miracles. We could spend all of our time trying to prove from a scientific reality whether a miracle could happen or not, but we could never really prove a miracle. Faith is never scientifically proven; it is neither rational nor irrational: it is trans-rational.

I believe this event actually happened, as there is nothing in the text that tells me otherwise. If God could raise Jesus from the dead in three days, he could preserve somebody alive in a fish. However, we don't want to miss the main point of this chapter by discussing the fish. The fish doesn't matter because the point of the story is not the fish, or even the prophet; **the point of the story is God** and the fact that God's steadfast love wins out and Jonah in his moment of desperation turns back to God.

In chapter 1, the captain said to Jonah, "Prophet man, shouldn't you be praying?" Jonah was not praying at that time because he was running from God. It was the pagan sailors at this point who led the way in prayer by praying to their gods. We are caught in a biblical paradox: the prophet is prayer-less and the pagans are prayerful! But now suddenly Jonah is alone and in trouble inside the fish—and *now* he prays. Near-death experiences have a way of quickening our prayer life.

This prayer has generated a lot of discussion amongst scholars. It is a theologically rich prayer and an eloquent prayer. Could the prophet have prayed this eloquently given his circumstances? And would he have later recalled the prayer so clearly? Perhaps Jonah reached into a known prayer from a prayer book of the day and he recited it word for word. In time of trouble, we often do this with the Lord's Prayer or with Psalm 23. Or perhaps the eloquence of the prayer is due to the practice of biblical writers looking back at critical moments when leaders prayed and enlarging upon or theologizing the prayer instead of recording it word for word. This latter explanation seems most likely to me.

Some scholars have even stated that the prayer is superfluous to the plot of the story, as we could go from 1:17 to 2:10 and not miss a beat in the moving narrative. But, since the author has added the prayer and the Holy Spirit has guided the process of it being included in Holy Writ, it must hold insight that is important to the story. It at least captures the theological import of prayer and even of a desperation prayer. Prayer is an essential aspect of our partnership with God. Take a moment and re-read the prayer slowly:

> *"I called out to the LORD, out of my distress,*
> *and he answered me;*
> *out of the belly of Sheol I cried,*
> *and you heard my voice.*
>
> *³ For you cast me into the deep,*
> *into the heart of the seas,*
> *and the flood surrounded me;*
> *all your waves and your billows*
> *passed over me.*

⁴ Then I said, 'I am driven away
from your sight;
yet I shall again look
upon your holy temple.'

⁵ The waters closed in over me to take my life;
the deep surrounded me;
weeds were wrapped about my head

⁶ at the roots of the mountains.
I went down to the land
whose bars closed upon me forever;
yet you brought up my life from the pit,
O LORD my God.

⁷ When my life was fainting away,
I remembered the LORD,
and my prayer rose to you,
into your holy temple.

⁸ Those who pay regard to vain idols
forsake their hope of steadfast love.

⁹ But I with the voice of thanksgiving
will sacrifice to you;
what I have vowed I will pay.

Salvation belongs to the LORD!"

Do you remember the last time you prayed a prayer asking to be rescued? It probably went something like this: **HELP!** The eloquence of the prayer is not what is essential. The essential element in the recording of this prayer is hearing the prophet cry out to God in desperation. Desperation adds intensity to our prayer life. Comfort is a prayer de-motivator. Desperation is a prayer motivator.

In looking at the first chapter of Jonah we explored how, in response to God's call to "get up and go," Jonah instead descended further and further. In this prayer, he repeatedly declares the spiritual and physical results of this downward movement of his:

"out of my distress . . . out of the belly of Sheol I cried" (v.2),

from *"the deep"* (v.2),

"the deep surrounded me" (v.5),

"at the roots of the mountains" (v.6),

"my life was fainting away" (v.7).

Jonah fled in a downward spiral until he reached a state of despair. The God that Jonah had wanted to escape had now become his only way out.

We hear surrender in the prophet's prayer. Upon hearing God's call, Jonah wanted to go his own way, and God let him go. God gave him a long rope, but eventually Jonah came to the end of that rope. When God calls us to challenging action, moving away from him might feel like a safer route, but such a path always leads to desperation, just as it did with Jonah. In his love, God will not manipulate us to follow his way, which leads to blessing, fruitfulness, and true identity. Instead, he extends an invitation and waits for us to accept it.

Jonah plunged himself into deep trouble as a result of his actions, but somewhere in his desperation he looked up to God. Prayer begins to turn the trajectory from downward plunge to upward victory:

"*I remembered the* Lord, *and my prayer rose to you*" (v.7).

"*yet you brought up my life from the pit* " (v.6).

Jonah was called to get up and go. However, he chose to go down. Now things were looking up again as the prophet looked up to his God. Desperation inspires us to look to God because we are finally moved to look beyond ourselves. Therefore, adversity can be one of the greatest gifts that can come our way because in those moments we finally look up to God.

I remember well one line of the prayer that my uncle prayed over Ingrid and me when we got married over thirty years ago: "*Lord give them enough success so that they don't lose hope and give them enough failure to keep their hands clinging to you.*" This is an amazing prayer, and I have prayed it over many people since that time. When we acknowledge God in the middle of our story, both success and failure can be places of thanksgiving and praise. Later in life we often reminisce over the challenging moments being the best moments.

If we did not have failure in our lives, we would eventually forget God. This cycle of forgetting God, falling into trouble, and then turning to God to find a way out is a pattern that is seen throughout the Scriptures and throughout history. C.S. Lewis said, "Pain insists upon being attended to. God whispers to us in our pleasures, speaks in our consciences, but shouts in our pains. It is his megaphone to rouse a deaf world."[1] Jonah was hearing again.

Jonah was definitely in pain. The most intense expression of anguish for Jonah is declared in verse 4:

"I am driven away from your sight."

Jonah felt as though he had been banished from God's sight. This is ironic because that is just what Jonah wanted to accomplish when he earlier ran from God's call. When he actually arrived at the felt sensation of separation from God he panicked. Feeling distant from God is the greatest anguish we can experience. The human spirit is amazing and can overcome amazing obstacles—if we have hope. God was Jonah's hope, but, having run from God, Jonah was now afraid that God had disappeared from his life for good, and if God had gone, so had Jonah's hope.

The plain descriptive nature of verse 5 is one of the reasons I like the word of God so much:

"The waters closed in over me to take my life;
the deep surrounded me;
weeds were wrapped about my head."

Only a biblical writer telling a real story while being guided by the Holy Spirit would throw such graphic detail into the biblical narrative. Jonah is facing imminent death. He is in the pit and life is ebbing away. Suddenly, there is this almost comic image of seaweed wrapping around his head. In the midst of this deeply theological construction of Jonah's prayer is this clear picture of the condition in this "safe place" for the prophet. It turns out that God has, in the belly of a great fish, created a holy temple for Jonah at the same time that Jonah is about to evoke God in his own holy temple.

The prophet moves the seaweed from his spiritual eyes to call out for rescue.

Verse 8 captures this shift in attitude and perspective:

> *"Those who pay regard to vain idols*
> *forsake their hope of steadfast love."*

In this powerful verse, Jonah recognizes that he has been clinging to a worthless idol, his own agenda, which has brought dissatisfaction and which has dragged him down: emotionally, spiritually, and literally. Now he wants to get back to God's grace. God's way now seems actually quite inviting.

The remembrance of the unchanging character of God reignited the hope of Jonah. God was known for His steadfast love—his *hesed* (חֶסֶד). That love wins out even in the face of the rebellion of his people. The Law declared it:

> *The LORD is slow to anger and abounding in steadfast love,*
> *forgiving iniquity and transgression* (Numbers 14:18).

The Psalmists repeatedly returned to the concept of God's steadfast love (mentioning it 127 times, in fact). In Psalm 40:11 we read some of the same ideas that Jonah expressed:

> *"As for you, O LORD, you will not restrain your mercy from me;*
> *your steadfast love*
> *and your faithfulness will ever preserve me!"*

The prophets also saw God's steadfast love as the motivating force to repentance:

> *Return to the LORD your God*, for he is gracious and merciful, slow to anger, and abounding in *steadfast love; and he relents over disaster* (Joel 2:13).

Verse 9 of Jonah 2 continues:

> *"But I with the voice of thanksgiving*
> *will sacrifice to you;*
> *what I have vowed I will pay.*
> *Salvation belongs to the LORD!"*

Having acknowledged God's love, Jonah next attempted to barter or negotiate with God. In chapter 1, pagan sailors made vows and now the wandering prophet makes his renewed vows. He wanted another opportunity to make the right choice: "Give me another chance, Lord, and I will do it right this time." We all do this—we try negotiating with God even when we do not really have anything to bring to the table. "Lord, get me out of this one, and I will do anything, even be a missionary to Africa."

Those vows are easily forgotten when the desperation passes. But the LORD is abounding in steadfast love. He rescues us for the sake of the relationship. Salvation belongs to the Lord!

Verse 10 brings the prayer to completion by showing an immediate result:

> *And the LORD spoke to the fish, and it vomited Jonah out upon the dry land.*

This rescue is kind of anticlimactic, isn't it? We expect a little more fanfare for the miracle that propels the prophet back into his calling. The miracle is vomit. Miracles are accomplished in the midst of the mundane and even the unspectacular. Maybe, as a result, we miss some of the most amazing miracles occurring around us. I expect the prophet to respond in praise or at least to kiss the dry ground because of God's reaching in and rescuing him. Instead, we end our theologically rich prayer with a pile of vomit and a rescued prophet.

Reading the book of Jonah in English, we can easily miss a powerful backdrop to the text because the Hebrew author uses different names for God. As mentioned earlier, the Hebrew Scriptures have multiple designations for God, but two primary words are used. The first is *Elohim* (מיהלא), usually translated as "God". It is the general name for God as Creator and Sustainer over all, the God of the nations. The second is Yahweh, pronounced *Jehovah* (הֹוהְי) and translated as LORD. This was God's intimate name, specially revealed through Moses to the Hebrew people. The Hebrews did not like when it was used in reference to other nations.

I think it is interesting that this prayer chapter begins with

Jonah praying to the "the LORD his God" (2:1). His original calling came from Yahweh. In fact, it is the favorite designation for God by the writer of Jonah's story—used twenty-six times in four chapters, with the largest number coming in chapter one. Now Jonah prays to Yahweh Elohim. And by the end of the story, it is Elohim who is speaking directly to Jonah to challenge his lack of love. And, more importantly, it is the LORD (Yahweh) who has pity on the great pagan city. Pagans too are to experience *hesed*, the steadfast love of Yahweh, the Israelites' special revealed name for God.

To our ears it feels as though the author is merely changing names to avoid redundancy, but that is not so. I do not believe that the ancient Hebrews would have liked this switch in the story. Yahweh is the special name of God, reserved for the use of the people of God and his prophets; Elohim is for the pagan nations. I do not want to get too far ahead in the Jonah story, but I want you to note that there is a back story being told in the shift in the names of God that are used in the progression of the Jonah story. This narrative is not only about the rescue of Jonah; it is about the rescue of the nations. And the backdrop message is for all of God's people throughout the ages: will we cling to a provincial, self-serving God, or will we be rescued from our myopic view of God, and join him in his project of love to restore the nations.

Jonah had been absorbed in his own world. His own anguish consumed him, and he couldn't think of other people. But God heard his feeble, self-centered prayer anyway because God was writing a larger story than just the story of Jonah. The God of steadfast love works a plan for nations, not just for one individual or one people. Whether you refer to him as Yahweh (the

LORD) or Elohim (God), he is coming at you with steadfast love. Thus, he may answer your less-than-noble prayer for a greater expression of that love. God loves regardless.

It is our prerogative, though, to decide whether or not we will allow God to rescue us and reposition us in the Restoration Project. He has given us freedom of will to respond or not— real love requires such freedom. Regardless of where we find ourselves—in the pit, on the wrong path, or in the belly of a fish—God invites us to a fresh start. The invitation is not to become a trophy for eternity. His rescue is an invitation back into the Restoration Project. Jonah is called once again to join God in rescuing others.

6

JONAH: A MAN BACK IN

THE RESTORATION PROJECT

1 Then the word of the LORD came to Jonah the second time, saying, 2 "Arise, go to Nineveh, that great city, and call out against it the message that I tell you." 3 So Jonah arose and went to Nineveh, according to the word of the LORD. Now Nineveh was an exceedingly great city-three days' journey in breadth. 4 Jonah began to go into the city, going a day's journey. And he called out, "Yet forty days, and Nineveh shall be overthrown!" [5] *And the people of Nineveh believed God. They called for a fast and put on sackcloth, from the greatest of them to the least of them.*

[6] *The word reached the king of Nineveh, and he arose from his throne, removed his robe, covered himself with sackcloth, and sat in ashes.* [7] *And he issued a proclamation and published through Nineveh, "By the decree of the king and his nobles: Let neither man nor beast, herd nor flock, taste anything. Let them not feed or drink water,* [8] *but let man and beast be covered with sackcloth, and let them call out mightily to God. Let everyone turn from his evil way and from the violence that is in his hands.* [9] *Who knows? God may turn and relent and turn from his fierce anger, so that we may not perish."*

[10] *When God saw what they did, how they turned from their evil way, God relented of the disaster that he had said he would do to them, and he did not do it.*

Repent! It sounds rather harsh. We don't like the idea of someone, even God, telling us what to do. We like our own way. However, as we have seen in the story of Jonah, our own way often leads us downward, away from God. Away from God is away from true identity and away from full purposefulness. So the call to repentance is an invitation back into the way of blessing. John Ortberg describes repentance in the following way:

"Repenting is a gift God gives us for our own sake, not His.
Repenting does not increase God's desire to be with us.
It increases our capacity to be with him."[1]

Notice how, through repentance, Jonah's life took a turn. Jonah got a second chance, and the story of Jonah moved immediately from a story about personal rescue and redemption to a story about the restoration of the nations. God's love for Jonah only makes sense when understood in light of God's love for all peoples and nations. His love is not exclusive; it is inclusive. And it is inviting. God invited Jonah back into the Restoration Project. Jonah was back in line with his life purpose to invite the Ninevites into Rescue.

We see in the story of Jonah's life a God of second, third, and even fourth chances; in fact, we know him personally as the God of innumerable chances. We are provided a picture of a God who is waiting patiently for us. He waits because he knows that we need him, not that he needs us. His love prompts him to continue to offer us what we need, no matter how long it takes for us to respond. St. Augustine, in his text *Confessions,* described our need for God in this way: "Our hearts are restless until we rest in God." The third chapter in the Jonah story describes a city that came to rest in this love of God, even when the prophet delivering the message of God's love was unsure that the city was worthy of hearing an invitation to repent, worthy of getting a chance to turn to God and receive his love.

INTERPRETATION OF JONAH 3

Verses 1-2 sound very familiar to us because they echo chapter 1:

> *Then the word of the LORD came to Jonah the second time, saying, "Arise, go to Nineveh, that great city, and call out against it the message that I tell you."*

Not all prophets need or receive a second chance at a missed calling. However, those of us who are stubborn often need a bit more convincing before we are ready to give up our own plans. Jonah certainly did. Jonah ignored the first calling from God and set off on his own, and from there things went from bad to worse for Jonah.

Jonah eventually returned to dry land, his place of comfort. There he heard God's call a second time. In this second call, we see God's great capacity for forgiveness: God makes no mention of the failed first calling. He doesn't bring up Jonah's past failures. He doesn't even try to use as leverage the vows that Jonah had made in his prayers (ch. 2). Nor does God remind Jonah that he was the one who had delivered Jonah, so that now Jonah owes him a greater debt. God simply and directly says, *Jonah, this is your calling: get up and go*.

Not everyone receives such a specific call from God, but for Jonah the picture was clear: he was to go to the great city of Nineveh. As mentioned earlier, Ninevah was the capital of Assyria, one of the most brutal and aggressive empires of the ancient world. The Ninevites were an archenemy of Israel and, therefore, of Jonah. Assyria had caused many problems for Israel in the past, and they would bring even more trouble for Israel in the future, even after encountering God through the prophet Jonah. They are mentioned again by the prophet Nahum, but this time in the context of judgment.

So why would God want to express Rescue to one of his people's enemies, particularly one that would cause even more problems for Israel in the future? Because it is the character of God to show compassion for ALL people. Any efforts to make him a provincial God cause us to miss the breadth of his love.

Jonah was called to preach to the enemy. In chapter 1 of Jonah, we read of God's words as they first intruded on Jonah's life:

"Arise, go to Nineveh, that great city, and call out against it."

In chapter 3, the call is given again; Jonah is to go to the great city of Nineveh and to . . .

"call out against it the message that I tell you."

The reiterated calling included the source of the message: it is God who is speaking. Jonah is to speak the message that God will give him—the *dabar* (רָבָד), the Word of God. It is not Jonah calling out to the Ninevites, but God calling out through Jonah. We are brought back to the main character of the story; it is not the prophet, it is not the great fish, it is not the great city—it is God, the storyteller!

The second time Jonah received the call, he obeyed and delivered the appointed message (verses 3-4):

> *So Jonah arose and went to Nineveh, according to the word of the LORD. Now Nineveh was an exceedingly great city three days' journey in breadth. Jonah began to go into the city, going a day's journey. And he called out, "Yet forty days, and Nineveh shall be overthrown!"*

Destruction is coming in forty days! What a message to hear. What a message to have to deliver, especially when it is given to one of your greatest enemies. "If you don't get right in forty days, you will be destroyed." This is not a message that we would expect to be received very well. But there is a sigh of relief that the prophet has finally gotten it right.

God gives the Ninevites some time to take in the message, though. He doesn't just strike. He doesn't say "tomorrow" or "next week" you will be overthrown. Jonah's message from God gives them "forty days."

Have you noticed how the number forty keeps appearing in the Scriptures? Noah waited forty days in the ark until the water went down. Moses spent forty days with God on the mount to receive the law, and his life is neatly divided into three sections of forty years. Ezekiel bore the sin of Judea for forty days. Jesus went out into the desert to fast for forty days. Forty is the scriptural number of completion, akin to saying *in God's time*, or in the perfect amount of time providentially assigned by God. Thus the message to Nineveh is a warning to repent in God's assigned time in order to experience his blessing. Repentance is an invitation to do life in God's way and in God's time.

Once they heard this message from God, delivered by the prophet Jonah, the people of Nineveh responded in a way that is surprising to any reader (verse 5):

> *And the people of Nineveh believed God. They called for a fast*
> *and put on sackcloth, from the greatest of them to the least*
> *of them.*

The prophet, who knew God, had heard his message and had initially gone in the opposite direction from God's plan, thus denying God. But these brutal pagan people responded immediately to this harsher message. **And with repentance!**

Somehow they hear that they are at enmity with and in rebellion against the living God, even though he is a foreign God to a people for whom they had little respect. They were hearing God—"they believed God" and not merely the prophet. Anyone wanting to be saved must begin at this point. People won't turn around—won't repent—until they acknowledge they are going in the wrong direction.

The Ninevites needed to change, and they did change, showing their change of heart by responding, not just inwardly, but also with outward signs of remorse: fasting and sackcloth.

The ancient peoples showed inner repentance (heart change) with acts of outward humiliation. Sackcloth was clothing that was made of coarsely woven fabric and was very uncomfortable; it was worn to remind the wearer of the condition of the heart that was not in a vibrant relationship with God. Fasting was a reminder not to be too comfortable with the things of this earth but to trust in God. Both actions were meant to express remorse from the heart and an intention for future change.

This news of God's message to Ninevah even arrived in the king's palace and he joined the outward acts of repentance (verse 6). He then made a decree to the entire nation:

> *"By the decree of the king and his nobles: Let neither man nor beast, herd nor flock, taste anything. Let them not feed or drink water, but let man and beast be covered with sackcloth, and let them call out mightily to God. Let everyone turn from his evil way and from the violence that is in his hands"* (verses 7-8).

Turn from evil and violence—radical for the Assyrians. This was a call for a comprehensive repentance, one that echoes that of Joel, another prophet of Israel, who called for a sacred assembly and a holy fast among the people of God. Ninevah's "pagan" king was even more exhaustive in his call than the prophet Joel. Not only were all people to fast, from the greatest to the least (v.5), but even the animals were to fast because the great city was in great trouble. The response of the king is so exhaustive that it is almost satirical. *Israel's enemies were responding wholeheartedly to God!*

The ancient audience of this narrative would not have missed this distinction between Jonah's response to God and the response of the Ninevites. It clashed with their cultural prejudices. Jesus would later tell a parable about the Good Samaritan that would likewise clash with the cultural prejudices of the Jews of his day. In the same way that the words "good" and "Samaritan" did not belong together in the minds of God's people, "repenting Ninevites" served as a staggering oxymoron to Jonah and his fellow Israelites.

Finally the king says, in verse 9:

> *"Who knows? God may turn and relent and turn from his fierce anger, so that we may not perish."*

Somehow this pagan king had a glimpse into the heart of God. His description of turning uses language similar to the language of repentance. The Ninevites needed to repent, to turn from their rebellion against God. Here the king is hoping that, as a result of their turning to God, God might turn ("repent") from his anger. He had not yet learned that God had no need to turn; he was already facing them, seeking them. It is always God pursuing us for relationship; it is we who turn our backs on God when we rebel. It is not God who turns.

The deeply theological hoping of the king becomes reality in verse 10:

> *When God saw what they did, how they turned from their evil way, God relented of the disaster that he had said he would do to them, and he did not do it.*

Elsewhere in Scripture we see this same emphasis on God's desire for all to be saved. II Peter 3:9 declares,

> *The Lord is not slow to fulfill his promise as some count slowness, but is patient toward you, not wishing that any should perish, but that all should reach repentance.*

We see it too in John 3:16, one of the first Scripture verses we memorize in Sunday school:

> *For God so loved the world, that he gave his only Son, that whoever believes in him should not perish but have eternal life.*

We often stop before verse 17, but we should read on:

> *For God did not send his Son into the world to condemn the world, but in order that the world might be saved through him.*

God's original design was for us to live in vibrant relationship with him, and in that relationship we find our ultimate purpose. But we rebelled, and the rest of the story of humankind is of us trying to recover that sense of purpose outside of God's pattern. Therefore, we trip and end up in trouble like Jonah or the Ninevites. Yet God is waiting for us to come back. Luke says it this way, *"there is joy before the angels of God over one sinner who repents"* (Luke 15:10). If this is true, how much more rejoicing is there when a city or a nation repents? Heaven celebrates the recovery of the original design of blessing—the Restoration Project.

We might think that the story is over at this point. And they lived happily ever after. We are certainly at a climax point. God rescues. But the storyline of the prophet is going to dip one more time. It will be the attitude and actions of the prophet in chapter 4 that bring the story to full climax for all of the people of God.

7

JONAH: A MAN'S HEART AND GOD'S HEART

THE CHALLENGE

1 But it displeased Jonah exceedingly, and he was angry. ² And he prayed to the LORD and said, "O LORD, is not this what I said when I was yet in my country? That is why I made haste to flee to Tarshish; for I knew that you are a gracious God and merciful, slow to anger and abounding in steadfast love, and relenting from disaster.³ Therefore now, O LORD, please take my life from me, for it is better for me to die than to live."⁴ And the LORD said, "Do you do well to be angry?"

⁵ *Jonah went out of the city and sat to the east of the city and made a booth for himself there. He sat under it in the shade, till he should see what would become of the city.* ⁶ *Now the* LORD *God appointed a plant and made it come up over Jonah, that it might be a shade over his head, to save him from his discomfort. So Jonah was exceedingly glad because of the plant.* ⁷ *But when dawn came up the next day, God appointed a worm that attacked the plant, so that it withered.* ⁸ *When the sun rose, God appointed a scorching east wind, and the sun beat down on the head of Jonah so that he was faint. And he asked that he might die and said, "It is better for me to die than to live."* ⁹ *But God said to Jonah, "Do you do well to be angry for the plant?" And he said, "Yes, I do well to be angry, angry enough to die."* ¹⁰ *And the* LORD *said, "You pity the plant, for which you did not labor, nor did you make it grow, which came into being in a night and perished in a night.* ¹¹ *And should not I pity Nineveh, that great city, in which there are more than 120,000 persons who do not know their right hand from their left, and also much cattle?"*

Every time we read or study the Bible we could benefit from asking three big questions. The first one is: **Who is God?** God is so large and beyond our imagination that we are constantly discovering and rediscovering aspects of him. The second question is **Who am I?** As we become familiar with who God is, we become better situated to know who we are. Our sense of identity is always clearer when we begin with what God says about us. His version of us is a crisper version. As we then grow in maturity, the identity question shifts from the singular to the plural: *Who are we?* Because life is not just about us individually, it becomes about the group. Finally, the third question is: *How does my/our life story fit into the story that God is telling?* Purposefulness and contribution flow more freely when we know how our daily assignments fit into his larger plan.

Let's quickly review the prophet's story to this point. God, in the middle of history, reached down to someone—his name was Jonah—and called him. The call was clear: *I want you to go and tell the people of Nineveh that I want to be in relationship with them.* Jonah the prophet ran in the opposite direction, because Nineveh was the capital city of Assyria, one of Israel's most brutal enemies. Yet God loved this prophet so much, and he loved these people of Ninevah so much, that he brought some interruptions into Jonah's plan. There was a great storm, and there was a great fish, and Jonah was rescued at the end of a great prayer. Jonah received a second chance to go to the great city to announce God's invitation. Here we receive an insight into God—he is the God of second, third, fourth, fifth, and more chances. The Ninevites heard the invitation and responded to God's call to turn their lives around to his more blessed way.

Now we come to the final chapter of the Jonah story, where we are once again surprised by the response of this confused and whiny prophet. The thesis and climax point of the entire narrative is found in the very final verse of the chapter, where God says, in so many words, *Should I not be concerned about this great city?* The implication is the unspoken message: *Jonah, my son, should you not also be concerned about this great city?* Jonah serves as a metaphor for all of us, all of the people of God throughout all of history, so this question is posed to us as well: Are we concerned about the things that concern God?

Has his heartbeat become our heartbeat? As we look at Jonah's life, we explore a little bit more deeply into our own spiritual journey of cooperating with the larger story that God is telling.

INTERPRETATION OF JONAH 4

Jonah chapter 4 opens with a surprising observation of the prophet:

> *But it displeased Jonah exceedingly, and he was angry.*

The text in the original Hebrew speaks of a fierce anger. The Hebrew *charah* (הָרָה) means *to burn with anger* or *to be furiously vexed*. We have heard this phrase before. The last time we heard about fierce anger was when the Assyrian king made a public declaration: *"God may turn and relent and turn from his fierce anger"* (3:9). The king had come under conviction; he had realized he and his people had rebelled against God, and he now expected a powerful God to respond to that rebellion with fierce anger.

But our story takes a turn, as it was not God who was angry at the end. His anger was set aside when the Ninevites repented. God's prophet, though, was burning mad. Jonah's anger is interesting because he had experienced God's steadfast love in his own life. Just a few chapters earlier, a great fish had consumed Jonah, so he had cried out to God, and God had answered him. Now Jonah is being consumed by his anger.

Not only was Jonah angry; he felt justified in his anger (verse 2):

*And he prayed to the LORD and said, "O LORD, is not this what
I said when I was yet in my country? That is why I made
haste to flee to Tarshish; for I knew that you are a gracious
God and merciful, slow to anger and abounding in steadfast
love, and relenting from disaster."*

This is an interesting reason for anger. He was angry because
God is gracious, compassionate, slow to anger, and abounding
in love. Doesn't that just make you mad when God acts that
way?

Jonah was struggling with the identity and nature of God.
He hadn't yet realized that God's identity was bigger than his
view of God. Jonah felt safe with his provincial and tribal God.
But God is the God of all people. We have similar struggles
today as we try to understand the nature of God. We often
want to reduce God to the elements of his character that make
us feel most comfortable.

For example, some people today want to distinguish
between the God of the Old Testament and the God of the New
Testament. They suggest that the God of the Old Testament
was angry, but somewhere in the course of history he got over
himself. They view the more self-realized God of the New
Testament as really loving and happy, smiling down on us. This
type of thinking keeps God amicable to us and we do not deal
honestly with his holiness.

The reality, though, is that God does not change (James
1:17). He remains the same, but because he reveals himself to
people within a particular time, place, and culture, he must
reveal himself in a way that will make sense to them. The God of
the New Testament wouldn't have made any sense to the people

of God in ancient times, within the epoch in which they lived. For example, in a world of competing deities, God revealed himself as the Warrior God. Many contemporary Americans want this notion banned from our thinking as an archaic reality. We want a safe God. The Warrior God is not safe.

This does not mean that his kindness, mercy, and love are missing in his self-revelation in the Hebrew Scriptures though. God brings holiness and love together in perfect harmony, which allows him to be both Lord of Hosts and Loving Heavenly Father at the same time. We even see these traits in his dealings with Jonah.

God's character has the capacity to act out perfect love with justice and execute justice with love. There is a complexity to his being that embraces holiness and justice even while he remains a God of mercy, love, and forgiveness. He cannot simply look at injustice and wink at it, though; that would be a denial of his just character. We wouldn't want a God like that. Something inside of us wants justice to be done—especially when someone we love has been wronged. This is the part of God Jonah wanted to see: God's justness expressed in his justice.

The desire for justice is reasonable; the problem is we don't operate with the same sense of justice that God does. Our view of justice is myopic, seen only from our own perspective. Even our application of justice is limited by the frailty of our human perspective. Our emotions can get in the way and turn justice into revenge. God, on the other hand, is not consumed by those emotions. Instead of using his anger to take revenge against those who have rebelled against him, God directs his anger toward the impact of sin in our lives. He sees us destroying ourselves, and he offers a better way for us. His anger is similar to that of a parent upon seeing a child miss great opportunities through bad choices. I have found that the question of the balance of God's justice and love is solved in the declaration that he is Good. I have to believe that a Good God knows how to perfectly blend and regulate the two. Chapter 4 of the Jonah story shows us that Jonah had not yet learned this truth.

We have no neat formula to deal with the complexity of God, and apparently Jonah didn't either. But any formula posed would have to account for the fact that God's mercy seems to win all the time. The loving nature of God is not just a New Testament reality. In Exodus 34, we read about when Moses received the law:

> And he passed in front of Moses, proclaiming, "The LORD, the LORD, the compassionate and gracious God, slow to anger, abounding in love and faithfulness, maintaining love to thousands, and forgiving wickedness, rebellion and sin. Yet he does not leave the guilty unpunished; he punishes the children and their children for the sin of the parents to the third and fourth generation" (NIV).

Here we see a God who holds us accountable with Law but showers us with love at the same time. God does what we are not capable of doing, of what we are not even capable of imagining. It is a mystery that his love and justice run freely together—and this mystery is bound up in his goodness.

In truth, Jonah was not really angry because God was loving. He was angry because God showed loving-kindness toward one of the enemies of his people. It's okay if God loves me; it's okay if God loves my people; but it is not okay for God to love the people who have brought so much trouble into my life and into the lives of my people.

Simply put, the prophet got God all wrong. Jonah was caught; his true heart was exposed. He started backpedaling and post-theologizing: *O LORD, is not this what I said?* I cannot help saying to the prophet: You weren't calling for a God of justice when you were in the belly of the great fish—then you were calling for a God of mercy and salvation!

We have likely heard of situational ethics. Here Jonah shows us a clear case of situational theology. Jonah adhered to one theology when he was in need and a different theology when he was in a more comfortable situation. We too want God to be certain things for us that we might not want him to be for others, especially for our enemies. I want a patient and understanding God who shows me mercy and grace. But I want the immediate justice and strong arm of the Lord for my enemies. I tend to trust my own "good" intentions, but easily interpret my neighbors' intentions as selfish. Maybe this is why Jesus tells us to deal with the planks in our own eyes before worrying about splinters in the eyes of others. Oddly enough, we miss the big planks for the glaring clarity of the tiny splinters.

Jonah continues his lament in verse 3:

> *"Therefore now, O LORD, please take my life from me, for it is better for me to die than to live."*

Ah, the whining prophet again. To be fair to Jonah, he is not alone in the tradition of whining prophets. Moses asked for death to avoid dealing further with the complaining Israelites. Joshua was leading the people into the Promised Land after forty years, and after just one setback, he joined the constant refrain of the people: *"Lord, it would have been better if we stayed in Egypt!"* (In other words, remember the good ole days when we were slaves?) Elijah dug himself into a state of depression and whining after one of his greatest victories demonstrating God's power at Mt. Carmel. Jeremiah is known to have had a good lament or two.

Have you ever whined? I have. I remember one faculty meeting in which I thought I had laid down a perfect argument for why the curriculum needed to change. One of my friends signaled to me to go outside. I expected a congenial moment where we would grab a Diet Coke or something, or where he would tell me what a great job I had done. But when we got outside he said, "Chuck, you are starting to sound like a whiner." Ouch! I was caught in my own cycle of complaint. I had failed to see the good that was all around, failed to see the opportunity to build a better curriculum. The issue was no longer the goal of attaining a better curriculum; it had become solely a desire to be heard and affirmed.

At the core of whining is ingratitude. Ingratitude is simply failing to recognize all the ways that God continually pours out blessing into our lives. Ingratitude disdains good for others, especially our enemies. When we get to this point, we get caught up in a vortex of negativity: ingratitude leads to whining and whining becomes the perpetual voice of ingratitude. Jonah, who had recently been given new life and a fresh start, had already forgotten his blessings; he had ceased being thankful to God.

T. A. Perry says about Jonah, "Jonah might possibly be the most persistently and intensely dejected characters in all of literature."[1] Though Jonah seems to have perfected the state of dejection, he is not alone in this, as a long line of prophets, and many of us, have found it easy to cross over into dejection. The only difference between Jonah and the other prophets is that the other prophets were disappointed in God because they thought God had not shown up for them. But Jonah was upset because God did show up. God had rescued him and God had given him success in his ministry. However, Jonah did not want success. Success meant that Jonah's enemies who repented would also experience the loving-kindness of God. Jonah was jealous: he did not want to share the blessings of God with anyone other than his own people, least of all with his enemy.

Jonah's whining moved to despair, and he then cried out, *"It is better for me to die than to live."* The Lord responds in verse 4,

"Do you do well to be angry?"

Translation: *Jonah, are you responding this way after I just showed you mercy? And after I used you to rescue a whole city?* Jonah was missing the whole point of the bigger story. His misunderstanding of God's plan led him to enter into a Job-like dialogue with God. Both Job and Jonah lamented their existence; both called out to die. But Job had had tragedies dumped on him; they were not a consequence of his own actions. Jonah, on the other hand, created his own problems because he chose a path away from God. Still, the end of the dialogue each had with God is basically the same: God challenged each man, "So what are you standing on in your complaint, and what is your vantage point to this whole situation?"

God to Job: "Job, where were you when I created the foundations of the earth?"

God to Jonah: "Jonah, what gives you a right to be angry?"

Jonah realized he could not win this argument. He would have to yield to God's plan, so he attempted to escape once again. Verses 5-6:

> *Jonah went out of the city and sat to the east of the city and made a booth for himself there. He sat under it in the shade, till he should see what would become of the city. Now the* LORD *God appointed a plant-and made it come up over Jonah, that it might be a shade over his head, to save him from his discomfort. So Jonah was exceedingly glad because of the plant.*

There are two words in this section of the story that are packed with meaning, words that would have grabbed the Hebrew listener. The first is the name for the little structure that Jonah built, which is called a *sukkah* (הָכֻּס). A *sukkah* was a flimsy structure. The word would have reminded the Hebrew listener of the Festival of Sukkoth, one of the three major festivals of Israel (Passover, Pentecost, and Sukkoth). The Scriptures refer to Sukkoth as the festival of tabernacles, or the festival of booths. Every year, for a period of time, the Israelites would build flimsy little structures (*sukkah*) that they would live in to remind themselves that God had rescued them from Egypt. They existed as a people because of the graciousness and steadfast love of the Lord to rescue them when they were strangers in a foreign land.

Interestingly, a major focus of the celebration of Sukkoth was the rereading of the Law, the Torah. In the Torah, specifically in Leviticus, God reminds Israel seven times that they are to show love to "strangers," a reference to foreigners and other peoples. Hebrew listeners would have grasped the Sukkoth connection at this point. Jonah in his *sukkah* was not giving thanks to God; he was neither remembering how God had rescued the Israelites nor how God had recently rescued him. Nor was he remembering the command of the Lord to show love to other peoples. Jonah was only complaining. He was flagrantly missing the point: the shelter was a reminder of past blessing—of liberation and salvation.

The question posed to us as we sit in our shelters of salvation (our *sukkah*) and read God's Word is *Will we remember how God has rescued us and, from that place of rescue, will we remember to show love to "strangers"?* Will we use the blessing of being saved to bless others unto salvation? Will the rescued and restored become partners with God in the Restoration Project?

The second word that would have struck a chord with early Hebrews refers to the shade (*tsel*, צֵל) that covered the prophet in his misery. The text makes it clear that God grew a vine over Jonah's head. Shade was a metaphor for God's covering. Isaiah 25:4 celebrates this image of God's care:

> *You have been our refuge, O God, a shelter in storm and shade*
> *for the heat.*

Jonah experienced both of those—shelter in storm and shade from the heat. Psalm 121:5 says,

> *"The LORD is your keeper; the LORD is your shade on your right*
> *hand."*

Jonah's little shelter became a place of comfort, and Jonah was happy. It is the only time in the story that we have a happy prophet. But self-centered prophets have short-lived happiness.

God is the ultimate provider; he provided the plant that gave Jonah shade. Then in his providence, he provided a worm that would destroy that same plant, thus taking away the shade. Why? Because as the ultimate provider, God was not primarily concerned about Jonah's comfort, he was concerned about Jonah's growth.

Verses 7-8:

> But when dawn came up the next day, God appointed a worm that attacked the plant, so that it withered. When the sun rose, God appointed a scorching east wind, and the sun beat down on the head of Jonah so that he was faint.

God provided a worm, a blazing sun, and a scorching east wind, and Jonah was no longer happy.

The prophet's lament to God just gets louder and more severe:

> And he asked that he might die and said, "It is better for me to die than to live."
> But God said to Jonah, "Do you do well to be angry for the plant?"

At this, Jonah became even more obstinate with God and pressed his case a bit further:

> "Yes, I do well to be angry, angry enough to die."

My response to the prophet is "Really? Why then did you, from within the large fish, cry out to the Lord to live?" But God is patient and slow to anger, even with a whining prophet. God loved Jonah so much that he would not leave him to wallow in his pool of self-pity. He counters self-pity with situations of discomfort.

In this episode, we once again see the power of adversity to shape our lives. The whole point of this scene is that God loved Jonah so much that he was not going to let Jonah dwell in comfort at the risk of misunderstanding his ultimate destiny. Jonah's life was part of a bigger story, a story that was bigger than what Jonah could see. God was willing to afflict Jonah in order to make him more aware of whom he was intended to be—an ambassador of God, a rescued bearer of loving-kindness.

John Ortberg describes the power of adversity in this way: "God isn't at work producing the circumstances you want. God is at work in bad circumstances producing the *you* he wants."[2] Ultimately, this *you* is really the *you* that you want as well. Once you return to your God design, you become fully alive, and you experience all of his joy and all of his purpose in the overflow of your life.

God showed his grace to Jonah by making him miserable, even though to Jonah it didn't feel like grace at all. In fact, Jonah felt so bad about his circumstances that he questioned life itself. Jonah had been given a second chance at physical life; now God was encouraging Jonah's spiritual life to catch up.

The story finishes with God's great words (verses 10-11):

And the LORD said, *"You pity the plant, for which you did not labor, nor did you make it grow, which came into being in a night and perished in a night. ¹¹ And should not I pity Nineveh, that great city, in which there are more than 120,000 persons who do not know their right hand from their left, and also much cattle?"*

God implies here **What about you? Shouldn't you be concerned as much about the people of Ninevah as you are for your own comfort?**

Thomas Carlisle's poem, "You Jonah," captures these questions so well.

*And Jonah stalked
to his shaded seat
and waited for God
to come around
to his way of thinking.
And God is still waiting for a host of
Jonahs in their comfortable houses
to come around
to His way of loving.*³

The main point of the Jonah story is revealed at this climax— once rescued will we use our new- found identity, freedom, and provision to join God proactively in his Restoration Project?

8

JONAH SUMMARY: MID-BIBLE CHECK-UP

THE STORY OF JONAH is strategically placed in the flow of the Bible to aid our understanding of the Big Story that God is telling. I see it as a mid-Bible check-up. God is the one performing the diagnosis of his people. Like any doctor, he is not being critical or antagonistic in addressing what is wrong or out of balance. His end goal is health for the patient. My physician may tell me in a routine visit that I am overweight and my blood pressure is high, and, as a result, I need to adjust my diet. He is not taunting me or being judgmental. He is being discerning and prescriptive for the end goal of my achieving good health. Likewise, the Great Physician gives his people a mid-course check-up through the narrative of Jonah's life. The diagnosis is not good, but there is always time for healing and renewal for his people.

In this light, the story of Jonah rests as a perfect reminder for God's people throughout the ages. Jonah's story is not only descriptive, it is prescriptive in the lessons learned and the underlying theological points of the story. The Apostle Paul wrote the following about the Hebrew Scriptures:

> *Now these things took place as examples for us, that we might not desire evil as they did* (I Corinthians 10:6).

> *Now these things happened to them as an example, but they were written down for our instruction . . .* (I Corinthians 10:11).

> *For whatever was written in former days was written for our instruction, that through endurance and through the encouragement of the Scriptures we might have hope* (Romans 15:4).

This midlife check-up and the resulting diagnosis are for our benefit. We reflect more deeply on these biblical accounts for the sake of our own health. We do not stop at reflection though. We move from reflection to action. Paul writes it this way:

> *Therefore, my beloved, as you have always obeyed, so now, not only as in my presence but much more in my absence, work out your own salvation with fear and trembling, for it is God who works in you, both to will and to work for his good pleasure* (Philippians 2:12-13).

Paul has stated it clearly: God is working out his will and good pleasure in and through us. This is the Story that God is telling. At the same time, we are called to work out our own salvation. This is the story that we are living. We should notice that the passage does not say to work *for* our salvation but to work *out* our salvation. We work out our salvation through continual endurance, reassessment, insight—and work! Underlying this admonition is an assumption of struggle and effort. Being invited into the Restoration Project does not seem natural, nor is it comfortable. Yet it is a second-level decision we must make in order to make the most out of our Rescue. We were bought with a price and then we proactively live out the value or worth of that redemption. It is an active salvation—I am not only **saved from**; I am **saved to**. I am saved to my destiny, my purpose, my full-fledged identity in Christ, and to my role in the Restoration Project.

So naturally, the text poses some questions to every rescued Christ-follower. Are we fully engaged in the Big Story? Are we proactively allowing our stories to merge with the plot line of God's Big Story? We will find that cooperation comes with a lot more fulfillment and blessing. If we choose not to cooperate, our stories will still be woven into the God story, but with a few more experiences of pain, disappointment, and frustration—and with a lot less fulfillment. Why? Because we were created for a purpose, and God is purposeful in telling his story (his story).

The following sections of this book will offer an expanded biblical understanding of the Big Story God is telling. The calling to and our purposeful engagement in the Restoration Project drips from every page of his Word and unfolds with every new chapter of history. As rescued ones we are chosen, called, commissioned, and celebrated in God's Word.

PART II

RESCUED FOR THE RESTORATION PROJECT: A CHOSEN PEOPLE

I HAVE DESCRIBED THE BOOK OF JONAH as a mid-course check-up for the people of God. Jonah is just one chapter in the larger story that God is telling. The underlying principles that flow from the Jonah narrative are not unique to the recounting of Jonah's experiences. These principles undergird the entire biblical account. Novelist Marilynne Robinson (quoted in Corn 1990) writes, "The great recurring theme of biblical narrative is always rescue, whether of Noah and his family, the people of Israel, or Christ's redeemed."[1] The drama is initiated in the action of God, who pursues his rebellious creation in love. The story unfolds in the choices we make to allow his love to embrace us or not. But the story is never complete at rescue. It is a continuum of rescue and restoration. The rescuers are chosen with renewed purpose to engage in the Restoration Project.

That initial rescue is called many things in scripture: redemption, salvation, adoption (back into the family of God), and new life, to note a few. The people of God are chosen. This notion of chosen-ness has been turned into a theological wrestling match at times, involving arguing points around predestination, free will, divine determinism, and sovereignty. But the Bible is about relationship far more than theological category and neat explanation. God's self-revelation and pursuit in love were never supposed to be turned into a theological puzzle to solve. The heart of God is about relationship. Relationship is always messy. We should always be wary of categorized or neat explanations of the nature of that relationship.

Behind this notion of chosen-ness (Rescue) is also invitation to be refitted for the Restoration Project. The historical observation of the people of God reveals that we have not always embraced this latter aspect of Chosen-ness. At times the people of God have interpreted chosen-ness from the angle of exclusivity. This has not been an intentional process but a reflex in security. Subtly, the people of God become self-consumed, caring for those already within the family to the point that they forget about those not yet in the family. However, the chosen people were not initially drawn into a private relationship with God but into one in which we are repurposed to invite others into his love. Rescue is always the first step, but it always leads to the second step—being employed in the Restoration Project.

Our sense of purposefulness is unlocked when we recognize that we are chosen to work alongside God in this movement. Being chosen is not a *carte blanche* to sit back and enjoy what we have been given. Instead, it is an invitation to partner with God to bring others back into God's original design. To better understand our own reactions to this invitation, we need to go back to the Big Story as described in the Bible to see how the status of being a chosen one has been a challenge for God's people throughout the ages.

Part II will unfold the biblical and historical realities of this two-part chosen nature. In the same way that God created a family to begin the story, and rebellion and the Fall began with that family, God initiated the beginning of Rescue through a new family. Chapter 8 will, from the Hebrew Scriptures (Old Testament), develop a biblical theology of the chosen people and their resulting mission. Chapter 9 will show how this chosen-ness of the Jewish family became the birthright of the people of God in the new family called the church. Chapter 10 will summarize the biblical notion of chosen-ness as primarily a relational theme of rescue and restoration. Chapter 11 will unfold how this struggle to live chosen-ness has developed through history, with implications for the contemporary family of God.

What we will discover in following this notion of chosen-ness through Scripture and on into history are the foundational aspects of a clear theology of mission. God is on mission—*Missio Dei*; out of his love he pursues his wandering children. Once rescued, we go on mission with him in the Restoration Project, pursing other wanderers. This is one of the major underlying themes of the larger story that God is telling in history.

Chosen-ness! Repositioned in family and repurposed in mission.

9

THE HEBREW PEOPLE OF GOD – CHOSEN

AT THE VERY CORE OF GOD'S CHARACTER is relationship. He has existed from eternity to eternity in Trinity: God the Father, Son, and Holy Spirit in continual dialogue and dance. He invites his creation into that continual discussion. Out of this aspect of relationship he has self-revealed in the language of family, the most fundamental and basic relational unit.

The opening story of creation is about the first family— a family established to collaborate with God and with one another in reigning over God's creation. This family is what we call humanity. This original family was the first to model our primary purpose: being co-creators with God, stewarding his gifts and authority (Genesis 1-2). Enter sin into the story (Genesis 3). With sin comes scarred identity, dysfunction in relationship, and struggle to find purpose in work. In spite of these, God did not give up on his struggling, dysfunctional creation, even though it continued in dysfunction.

This human family struggled to such a degree that it was eventually splintered into multiple families (nations) and was scattered around the world to keep it from the worst of idolatries—trying to be like God. The human families had become so dysfunctional, so resistant to God's plan, that they tried to make names for themselves rather than allowing God to make a name for them (Genesis 11). From this point forward, the Bible tells the long and continuing story of God calling his splintered and scattered families back into relationship with himself and with each other.

Scripture shows us right from the beginning that God chooses to work in partnership with his creation so, when he established this fresh start, he initiated a rescue plan through one family—that of Abram. He did so with a new covenant, in which he promised to make Abram's family great—more numerous than the grains of sand and the stars in the sky. The story of this new beginning started with the call to Abram (Genesis 12), and it was ratified in covenant (Genesis 15), where Abram was renamed Abraham by God.[1] If we pay close attention to the context of the call, we notice a clue to what God was up to—he was intimating that he is not just the Father of one great family; he is a Father of many families—and the Father of the nations:

> *Now the LORD said to Abram, "Go from your country and your*
> *kindred and your father's house to the land that I will show*
> *you. And I will make of you a great nation, and I will bless*
> *you and make your name great, so that you will be a blessing.*
> *I will bless those who bless you, and him who dishonors you*
> *I will curse, and in you **all the families of the earth** shall*
> *be blessed"* (Genesis 12:1-3).

God declared that Abram would be his special agent. He would be blessed, not just to bathe in his good fortune, but to live out a purpose: to be a blessing to others! This dual nature of blessing is often expressed by the phrase "blessed to be a blessing." This is a key declaration, one we must take note of if we are to understand the full nature of chosen-ness. Being chosen is not the result of something special in us. It is the initiative of God, often in spite of ourselves. Jonah was clearly a story in this vein.

We might be tempted to give Abraham hero status because he is called the father of faith. Yet, as we read the story of father Abraham, the human father of faith, we see a man who got it all wrong a number of times and all right a few times. Regardless, he could not escape favor and success because God had chosen to bless him. It was God who initiated the relationship. Abram hadn't chosen God; God had chosen Abram. More importantly, the blessings God chose to bestow on Abraham were not to stop with Abraham. He was not to be an accumulator of blessing, but a multiplier of blessing. **Blessed to *be* a blessing!** Therein lies the crux of chosen-ness.

"Blessed to be a blessing" may be a concept that is foreign to some. As humans we have an instinct to be accumulators.

Blessing is good. It is natural to want more of it. And there is nothing wrong with wanting more of it. However, it is easy to get to a point in life where we hoard blessing, even spiritual blessing. We forget that God's blessing is unlimited. We refrain from sharing it with others, fearing that doing so will leave us with less. We forget that God disperses blessings to us so that we may share with others, that he blesses us so that we will be a blessing to others. He does not want us to accumulate selfishly, and he especially does not want us to accumulate spiritual blessing. He wants us to use that place of favor to pass on the blessing to others who have less. Blessing wastes away when we clutch it. When it is given away, blessing has exponential power both for giver and the receiver.

As we read on in the story of Abraham, we are amazed at the dysfunction of this family and at their inability to pass the blessing on to others. Abraham's sons, grandsons, and great-grandsons, and all their wives, were unlikely ambassadors for God. These earthly fathers were spiritually passive, the mothers were conniving, and the sons and daughters were deceptive, jealous, and rascally. They resembled the first family after the Fall. Even so, they give us courage in the midst of our own dysfunction and imperfections because we come from similar families.

Despite their inability to fulfill God's purpose, God continued to work out his plan to restore humankind through them. For example, God placed a marker in Abraham's family line—a new name that showed that God was preparing for a new stage of the story. A moment of wrestling with God resulted in Jacob, a grandson of Abraham, being renamed Israel (Genesis 32), establishing him as one chosen by God. When the families of the world became dispersed by sin at the tower of Babel, God chose to use this newly selected family, this new nation Israel, the family of Hebrews, to restore all the families, all the nations, back to God's covenant blessing.-

God then wrote the next chapter in his Big Story of restoring the nations: one of Jacob's sons (a great-grandson of Abraham) was carried off to Egypt. His name was Joseph. His life took many crazy turns, but, through it all, God continued to show him favor in this new nation. Joseph summarized his life with these words:

> "...it was meant for evil but God turned it to good for the saving of many" (Genesis 50:20).

The twists in Joseph's story were a forewarning that God would bring his blessing through some unusual ways, including through the unfortunate and ungodly activities of a dysfunctional covenant family and through the oppression of one of the dispersed families (nations).

In the next chapter of the Big Story, the purposefulness and the blessing of God are not obvious to the casual observer. The new family Israel became a new nation, but they also became slaves. How could a nation reduced to slavery become a blessing to other nations? And how can one say that this nation of slaves was experiencing the favor of God? Scripture tells us the answer to both questions:

> But the people of Israel were fruitful and increased greatly; they multiplied and grew exceedingly strong, so that the land was filled with them (Exodus 1:7).

Things are not always as them seem. I like to refer to what we see of our lives as *text*. What we do not see immediately, but occasionally see later with hindsight, is *subtext*. Behind the text of our lives God is telling a Bigger Story. **Life unfolds with text *and* subtext.**

Interestingly, as the chosen family of God grew in number, their situation grew more desperate: from slavery to more severe oppression and even on to the mass murder of their sons by the slave owners. This hardship went on for a long time: four hundred years (Exodus 12:40-41). God was loudly silent at this time, so it is hard to believe that this period was part of the storyline in God's Bigger Story. But then we hear this declaration in the Word that makes the silences of God seem a bit less arbitrary:

> *During those many days the king of Egypt died, and the people of Israel groaned because of their slavery and cried out for help. Their cry for rescue from slavery came up to God. And God heard their groaning, and God remembered his covenant with Abraham, with Isaac, and with Jacob. God saw the people of Israel—and God knew* (Exodus 2:23-25).

The people of Israel cried out. God had heard them all along, though at the time, his silence might have been interpreted as a lack of attention. God's actions always tie into a mysterious larger story, a story that often does not make sense to us or does not seem evident to us at a particular moment in time, but one that becomes much clearer with hindsight. The Spanish mystics captured it well: "God draws straight with crooked lines." Such is the case with the story of the Israelites in Egypt. And such is the case with all of our stories.

And **God heard** their groaning.

And **God remembered** his covenant with Abraham.

And **God saw** the people of Israel—and **God knew.**

We also see that **God acted**. God prepared a liberator on the inside of the Egyptian system—Moses: blessed by God, Hebrew-born, but raised in privilege in Pharaoh's courts (Acts 7:22). Moses started out as a wannabe liberator, one with an idea of the ancient covenant—blessed to be a blessing! But he acted in his own power and ended up herding sheep in the wilderness. For eighty years God worked to prepare Moses to declare His words: "Let my people go!" Forty years in Pharaoh's courts and forty years in obscurity. Then, after this preparation, God was ready to use Moses, and his brother Aaron, to make himself known to the people of Egypt:

> *"And the Egyptians will know that I am the LORD..."* (Exodus 6:7, 14:4).

There is a mysterious aspect to the Big Story that needs to be addressed at this point. Why does God take so long? Years of slavery. Years of preparing a liberator. Years of waiting for a redemption answer in a Messiah. Years of giving Satan and the kingdom of darkness a long leash. Years of a church struggling to bring the gospel to all nations.

Frankly, I do not know why God takes so long. From what we can see, God is not in a hurry to finish his story. Scripture is helpful to us again at this point:

> *"But do not overlook this one fact, beloved, that with the Lord one day is as a thousand years, and a thousand years as*

one day. The Lord is not slow to fulfill his promise as some count slowness, but is patient toward you, not wishing that any should perish, but that all should reach repentance" (II Peter 3:8-9).

Simply put, God's clock operates at a different pace than our clocks. Ultimately, though, the bottom line is quite encouraging: what appears to us to be slowness is actually God's patience, giving us an opportunity to reach repentance. And for all to join the Restoration Project.

Let's return to the Big Story. God liberated the slave family (Exodus 12) in a fantastic story involving death, blood, being marked, liberation, and a new start. (All of these were symbols of the ultimate Rescue.) For the moment in the Story, the God family was free. The family had grown through God's blessing and had become a nation. What is fascinating in the story is that once they were free the struggle of walking into their new purpose was so challenging that the rescued nation longed to go back to slavery.

By Exodus 19, God had reiterated the identity and purpose of this family. The people of God had been chosen as ambassadors to the nations, the other not-yet peoples of God. It is true that God called the renewed family of Israel a "treasured possession" (19:5), but this distinction had nothing to do with how special they were in themselves. God had to repeatedly remind them of this:

"It was not because you were more in number than any other people that the LORD set his love on you and chose you, for you were the fewest of all peoples" (Deuteronomy 7:7).

Rather, through them God was continuing his passion to restore all nations (all dispersed families), and his project was to begin through a covenant with this one nation (one family). They were being blessed to be a blessing. Hear the words:

> *"And you shall be to me a kingdom of priests and a holy nation"*
> (Exodus 19:6).

They were being called to be a priestly kingdom. The role of a priest was to serve as mediator between the people and God. This priestly people were to be a mediator between the peoples of the other nations and God.

Again in the story we are met with the question of whether or not the chosen nation would step up to its chosen role. Sadly, the people saw their chosen-ness as a matter of exclusivity. They became blessing-hoarders, not multipliers. God did not abandon them, though. Through the prophets in the following years, God kept calling his chosen people back to his original design. Here are some of these declarations:

> *"I am the LORD; I have called you in righteousness; I will take you by the hand and keep you; I will give you as a covenant for the people, a light for the **nations**"* (Isaiah 42:6).

> *"I will make you as a **light** for the **nations**, that my salvation may reach to the end of the earth"* (Isaiah 49:6).

In fact, the nations are mentioned 431 times in the Hebrew Scriptures, making it a prominent theme. Israel, the first family, was to live out her purpose in the context of the nations. Her blessing was to be the blessing of the nations and of the peoples of the earth (Psalm 67). But she struggled with this aspect of chosen-ness. Our prophet Jonah became the living metaphor of this struggle.

Israel never did get totally on board with their calling, but God continued to use them as part of his plan, even in their downfall as a nation. Because they did not act as ambassadors to the nations, God allowed the nations to overtake them. The people of God became slaves again and were carried away from their land. This diaspora was God's way of helping them to continue to play a part in the Big Story. They involuntarily became ambassadors.

Two things happened in this dispersion that set up the next chapter of God's revelation to all nations (which was still a few hundred years off). First, worship of the Living God was decentralized from Jerusalem. After a number of generations, the dispersed family realized that it might not get back to Jerusalem for a long time. Their generations born in these foreign lands were going to forget the way of Yahweh. So the displaced people began building multiple places of worship, called synagogues. Whereas Jerusalem had been the place to worship God, now God had seats of worship out among the other nations. The once provincial God moved internationally, and he did so by using the original covenant nation. Actually God was always international; he was just waiting for his partner family to join him in this. With this move, other families and nations had much greater access to the worship of the Living God, the Creator and Redeemer of all peoples.

After many generations in exile, not only had the hope of Jerusalem become distant, the mother tongue of the original covenant family had been lost. New generations wanted to assimilate into their new locales and so, over time, they abandoned the Hebrew language. As a result, the second important event arising from the dispersion occurred: the Word of God was translated into Greek. (This translation is called the Septuagint.) This step was important because Greek was the lingua franca of the Mediterranean Basin, connecting many different cultures and peoples.

When the Hebrew Scriptures were translated into Greek, the Word of God became accessible not only to the dispersed family, but also to the peoples with whom they had assimilated. Previously, God had been inaccessible through his written Word to those who didn't understand Hebrew because God's revealed *written* message was only in Hebrew. Most people could only know God's character through the general revelation of creation. With the Greek translation, though, God became even more accessible, and thus more understandable, through the special revelation of his Word.

As the dispersed people lived righteous and honorable lives among the nations, other nations were drawn into worship of the Living God. Those new worshippers in the Mediterranean Basin became known as God-fearing Greeks, or simply God-fearers. God's chosen people had unwillingly and unwittingly fulfilled their purpose as ambassadors.

The largest piece of the Hebrew story was yet to unfold. The promise of God was that out of the nation of Israel would come the one who would be the Lord of all nations, as promised in a messianic Psalm:

The LORD *said to me, "You are my Son;*
today I have begotten you.
Ask of me, and I will make the nations your heritage,
and the ends of the earth your possession" (Psalm 2:7-8).

He was not to be the Messiah for only one people but Messiah for all peoples. For all nations! The Savior of the World! His coming had been announced early on through Abraham in the covenant blessing of nations. It was reaffirmed in the Exodus declaration of the chosen people as a priestly nation. The prophets and the psalmists reiterated the calling, and the prophet Jonah himself became a living image of the struggle of the calling. Chosen-ness!

But once again there would be a long period of waiting. The people would be in exile and diaspora for hundreds of years before this Messiah, the Son and Savior would appear. That chapter would be the turning point of the Big Story.

10

THE CHURCH: THE NEW CHOSEN FAMILY

THE BIG STORY TURNED with God's action of Incarnation. The eternal Son shed his robe of glory (Philippians 2:5-11) to make God more accessible in revelation. He was the exact representation of the glory of God (Hebrews 1:3). Jesus, the Christ (Messiah), the unique Son, became the guarantor of the covenant fulfillment. This chapter is the most important chapter in the Big Story. All the rest of the chapters hang on this chapter. Yet each chapter was, in itself, important in leading up to this chapter.

When we step back, we see that God was guiding, ever so

subtly, the very movements of his people. In his Sovereignty he did not manipulate. He led by invitation first. He invited them to participate freely, to voluntarily live out chosen-ness. When they stalled, he helped them by scattering them. In it all, God desired to be reconnected to all the families of the earth. The apostle Paul would later declare this truth while preaching to the Athenians:

> "God…made from one man every nation of mankind to live on all the face of the earth, having determined allotted periods and the boundaries of their dwelling place, that they should seek God…and find him…" (Acts 17:26-27).

Creation. Fall. Rescue. Restoration. In Jesus, rescue was settled once for all. The required yearly sacrifice for atonement was now eliminated through a once-for-all sacrifice (Hebrews 9-10). Slaves to sin were not only set free, they were adopted fully into the God-family (Romans 8:15). The rescue came with a new sense of urgency for engagement in the Restoration Project. Jesus modeled this urgency from the moment he began his earthly ministry. He included the Gentiles in his pursuit—to the surprise of the Jewish leaders and even, at times, to the surprise of his disciples. They still had the myopic vision of Jonah. Jesus, the Son of Man, had come "to seek and save the lost" (Luke 19:10).

The gospel writers capture well this difference between the perspective of Jesus and that of the established religious leaders. Mark contrasts the lack of faith of the Jewish leaders and of the Jewish community with the great faith of the pagans. Matthew shows Jesus correcting Pharisees, while ministering to Gentiles. Luke points to Jesus's penchant for the marginalized and the distant. John recounts Jesus passing through Samaria, unclean territory, and engaging a woman at a well. Religious leaders of the time usually went around Samaria, but Jesus was a boundary-crosser: he entered right into the other "nation's" territory. He was simply living out his purpose as the "sent one." Jesus refers to himself over forty times as the "sent one." He was sent by the Father to cross the boundary between heaven and earth in his incarnation. Once on earth, he crossed geographic, social, cultural, and religious boundaries for the sake of making the love of God accessible to those who were regularly held in disdain by the religious inner circle.

Jesus was unambiguous in the action plan he gave to his followers. We might call his followers the *first family, thirdly chosen*. The first chosen family of Adam and Eve failed to fulfill its God-given purpose. The second chosen family of Abraham also failed. The church then became the new family of God, its members again chosen not in an exclusive way, but in a purposeful way. To his followers, Jesus reiterated this role of the chosen people in the Restoration Project through what we today refer to as the Great Commission:

> "*As you are **going**, make disciples of all nations…*" (Matthew 28:18-20).

> "*As the Father has sent me, so **send** I you…*" (John 20:21).

> "*I do not pray that you take them out of the world but that you keep them from the evil one…as you have sent me into the world, even so **I am sending them** into the world…*" (John 17:15, 18).

*"You will receive power when the Holy Spirit comes upon you and you will be my **witnesses** in Jerusalem, Judea, Samaria, and **to the ends of the world**... "* (Acts 1:8).

The next chapter of the Big Story is the church's struggle, as the newly formed people of God, to live out the dual nature of chosen-ness.

The new family is called the church, the new covenant people of God. The sons and daughters of God, and the brothers and sisters of Jesus, become the new agents to fulfill the God-call to invite all the dispersed families back into relationship with God. These are the nations (εθνοσ, in Greek not the "nation state" as we think but ethnicities, or culturally distinct peoples) to which Jesus was sending his followers (Matthew 28:18-20). However, the early church initially made the same mistake as the earlier covenant families, interpreting chosen-ness as exclusivity rather than purposefulness, forgetting to be distributers of blessing.

When Jesus gave the call in Acts 1:8, he told the disciples to return to Jerusalem and wait for the gift of the Holy Spirit, who would empower their efforts as boundary-crossing witnesses—witnesses to Jerusalem, Judea, Samaria, and the ends of the earth. Though they received the Holy Spirit, they struggled to embrace the call.

They did have great success among their own people, and the church grew explosively in Jerusalem. Interestingly, the first wave of conversion was among the Hellenists—dispersed Jews visiting Jerusalem on Pentecost (Acts 2). When Peter preached on the day of Pentecost, three thousand came to the faith. In Acts 2:42-47 we are told the Lord added to the number of believers daily. In the story of the church as recorded in the Acts of the Apostles, two phrases frequently appear: "they increased in number" and "the Word of the Lord increased." This increase is reminiscent of what the people of God experienced in Egypt: multiplication and great growth.

But this initial growth remained inward and local. The new family was stuck. So God used a time-tested method to help them back on the path of restoring all nations—involuntary dispersion. The new family experienced significant persecution. Then one day, one of their key orators, Stephen was martyred while preaching (Acts 7). As a result, the people of God scattered:

> And they were scattered throughout the regions of Judea and Samaria (Acts 8:1).

God's hand in this movement would have been questionable to those early Christ-followers. How could the death of one of their key leaders and best orators help the advancement of God's message? The subtext of what was transpiring became clearer just three verses later:

> Now those who were scattered went about preaching the word (Acts 8:4).

What the believers were unwilling to do voluntarily, God helped them to do through struggle and dispersion. The calling of Acts 1:8 is manifested in this dispersion—Jerusalem, Judea, Samaria.

There is one more important element in the story of Stephen

and the distribution of God's invitation to the nations. It was Saul, who led the martyrdom of Stephen and the persecution against the church, which then led to the dispersion (Acts 7-8). Saul had his own revelation moment (Acts 9). On the road to Damascus, as he sought to do more damage to the new family of God, he was knocked off his horse by a bright light. In that moment, the resurrected and ascended Jesus spoke directly to him. Saul was blinded and, while he was convalescing in Damascus, the Lord sent to him a man named Ananias, to be an agent of healing for Saul's eyes, both physical and spiritual. Saul was given a new calling in life. Rather than continuing as persecutor of the new family, he became a part of that family and its most aggressive and proactive agent of invitation to the nations. God first revealed his plan for Saul by telling it to Ananias:

"Go, for he is a chosen instrument of mine to carry my name before the Gentiles..." (Acts 9:15).

Chosen-ness! Purposefulness! Saul was chosen and called in one moment. He was to become ambassador for the God of the nations!

The change of calling for Saul also brought a change in name. Saul became Paul. Paul became an agent of God, inviting the nations to be reunited with God in vibrant relationship. Now, for the first time in the Big Story, the people of God proactively embraced and acted on their chosen purpose (Acts 13). They went voluntarily this time, not needing God's push through dispersion. The Holy Spirit-inspired and -saturated movement went global.

If we read this story of Paul and Barnabas in light of God's larger story, we will find some interesting connections that show that God's purpose and plot are more far reaching than we can sometimes see. When we look back at what happened when the Israelites were dispersed among the nations, we see that God's actions at the time of the Old Testament dispersions and the results of those actions continued to be the platform for the spread of God's message, even in New Testament times. The Old Testament dispersions had given rise to synagogues, which had decentralized worship, moving it out of Jerusalem and into the nations. Interestingly, the synagogue would also become instrumental in the church's outreach to the nations. Paul and Barnabas, the first proactively sent missionaries of that church, initially followed a strategy of beginning their mission work in these synagogues, proclaiming and demonstrating the truth of this God as revealed completely in Jesus.

Remember too that during these earlier dispersions, the Word of God was translated into Greek, thus making it accessible to the nations. As a result, many God-fearing Greeks and Jewish Hellenists were added to the group of peoples that knew the Living God. Paul was a Pharisee, so he knew the Scriptures inside and out, and he likely knew those Scriptures in the Hebrew language. In fact, Paul describes himself as a "Hebrew of Hebrews" (Phil. 3:5). It cannot be coincidence that this Paul, whom God would use mightily to spread his message to the nations, grew up in Tarsus, where he also learned to speak *koine* (common) Greek. Just as Moses had been raised in an Egyptian court to prepare him to communicate to Pharaoh, Paul grew up in a Greek context to prepare him to be an ambassador to the nations.

During his earthly ministry, Jesus had made it clear that

the purpose of this new chosen family, the church, was to reach out to the other families of the earth. The underlying tension in the Acts of the Apostles was whether this new family would actually fulfill this purpose. Why was it so hard for them to do this? Simply put, they were ethnocentric or *their-own-people-centric*. Take, for example, Peter. Under the power of the Holy Spirit, he preached effectively, inviting thousands in from his own people. Yet, even he needed a second revelation to believe that Gentiles were truly welcome as part of the extended family of God. Peter received a vision of a sheet lowered from heaven with unclean animals on it and was told to eat (Acts 10). This revelation baffled Peter until he heard God's word, *"Don't call unclean what I call as clean."* In other words, God was telling Peter, don't hold Gentile, pagan families at a distance. They are potential full-fledged brothers and sisters in the family of God.

After this revelation, Peter was used by God to invite a God-fearer by the name of Cornelius and his biological family into the family of blessing. This event was so monumental that Luke used two chapters to tell and then retell the story. It was not just about the saving of a non-Hebrew family. The recounting is importantly capturing Peter's second-level conversion (Acts10-11). He was moving from being a people of God blessing-hoarder to a people of God blessing-dispenser. Peter was losing his Jonah-shaded worldview.

Peter then returned to the stalled church in Jerusalem to once again make clear God's intention. Blessed to be a blessing; Chosen for a purpose. But the church still struggled with this idea, so much so that they held the first Church Council (Acts 15) in order to discuss whether Gentiles would be fully embraced in the new family and to discuss which of the Jewish traditions they would have to uphold to remain as upstanding family members. This was the historical tension felt by the church. Freshly visited by the resurrected Christ with his message to "go, make disciples of all nations" (Matthew 28:18-20) and freshly baptized in the Holy Spirit (Acts 2), the church still needed a second-level conversion to embrace their partnership with God in mission.

Paul, the missionary, understood this tension and continually pushed the boundaries, literally and figuratively. His words captured his own proactive stance in this effort,

> *"I have become all things to all people so that by all possible means I might save some"* (I Corinthians 9:22).

In fact, it put him in tension with Peter and the Church Council at different times (Galatians 2). This ongoing conflict, even in the early church, was a foreshadowing of the ongoing tension that the church would face throughout history. Will we live in mission toward others or succumb to the reflex to remain inward with our own people?

The apostle Paul most clearly expressed this theology of going in his letter to the church in Rome:

> *"For 'everyone who calls on the name of the Lord will be saved.' How then will they call on him in whom they have not believed? And how are they to believe in him of whom they have never heard? And how are they to hear without someone preaching? And how are they to preach unless they are sent? As it is written, 'How beautiful are the feet of those who preach the good news!'"* (Romans 10:13-15).

Here the church is clearly described as the proactive sender in missions. Good news required a herald. The herald was to be proactively sent by the church.

One last image from Peter reminds the church of how this chosen-ness was passed down from the original family/nation (Israel) to the new family/nation (the Church).

> *"As you come to him, a living stone rejected by men but in the sight of God chosen and precious, you yourselves like living stones are being built up as a spiritual house, to be a holy priesthood, to offer spiritual sacrifices acceptable to God through Jesus Christ"* (I Peter 2:4-5).

> *"But you are a chosen race, a royal priesthood, a holy nation, a people for his own possession, that you may proclaim the excellencies of him who called you out of darkness into his marvelous light. Once you were not a people, but now you are God's people; once you had not received mercy, but now you have received mercy"* (I Peter 2:9-10).

> *"Keep your conduct among the Gentiles honorable, so that when they speak against you as evildoers, they may see your good deeds and glorify God on the day of visitation"* (I Peter 2:10).

The language is strikingly parallel to that found in Exodus 19. The new people of God are described as a **priestly people, a nation**, gathered together to be light to the **other Gentile nations**.

Even though the family has struggled at times to embrace

that call, the Scriptures give us a vision at the end of the story through a look into the future throne room of God, where all the peoples, all the families, are gathered in worship reunion:

> *And they sang a new song, saying,*
> *"Worthy are you to take the scroll*
> *and to open its seals,*
> *for you were slain, and by your blood you ransomed people for God*
> *from every tribe and language and people and nation,*
> *and you have made them a kingdom and priests to our God,*
> *and they shall reign on the earth"* (Revelation 5:9-10).

Once again the language is strikingly familiar, echoing the expressions of Exodus 19 and I Peter 2: *"a kingdom and priests to our God, and they shall reign on earth."* Not only are the worshippers described as coming from every tribe, language, people, and nation, they are connected to the ancient calling for all of eternity. The story comes full circle as the families of the earth now rule with God, as was intended in his original design, and live out their priestly kingdom role.

11

A BIBLICAL SUMMARY OF CHOSEN-NESS

RESCUE AND RESTORATION

IN THE BIBLICAL TEXT, being chosen is a concept of emphasizing God's initiative in our relationship. In the Hebrew Scriptures it is applied most clearly to the people of God as a collective group, as opposed to an individualistic understanding. Deuteronomy, the fifth book of the Bible, establishes clearly the concept of chosen-ness. This emphasis of divine initiative makes perfect sense in light of the covenant backdrop of Deuteronomy. God was the initiator and guarantor of covenant relationship with his people. Though this chosen nature is noted several times (Deuteronomy 4:37, 10:15, 14:2), Deuteronomy 7:6-7 is a crystalized statement of the identity of the nation of Israel as a chosen people:

> *"For you are a people holy to the LORD your God. The LORD your God has chosen you to be a people for his treasured possession, out of all the peoples who are on the face of the earth. It was not because you were more in number than any other people that the LORD set his love on you and chose you, for you were the fewest of all peoples."*

Chosen-ness was not due to the quality of the one chosen. God could have chosen a larger or more impressive-looking people to serve as his agent. Chosen-ness was rooted in the love and selection of God.

This chosen-ness is declared again and again throughout the narrative of God's people in the Hebrew Scriptures. Israel, as a people and as a nation, was chosen (I Chronicles 6:13; Psalm 105:6; Isaiah 41:8-9; Ezekiel 20:5). The emphasis is always on the initiative of God and his guarantee of the relationship. However, it is also a reminder that the chosen nature is always accompanied with the calling to serve as his agent to the other nations.

The story was recorded for the people in their holy books, later collected in one Holy Book, known to Christians as the Old Testament. It was to remind the people that they had been chosen by Yahweh to be God's promise of healing and restoration to the fractured family of humanity now divided into clans of hostility called nations. Chosen always had purposefulness as its subtext, not exclusivity.

The culmination of this chosen assignment is found in the prophetic expectations of the Messiah who would come to bring

God's order. Isaiah 42:1 declares:

> *"Behold my servant, whom I uphold, my chosen, in whom my*
> *soul delights; I have put my Spirit upon him; he will bring*
> *forth justice to the nations."*

Note how this chosen-ness has impact beyond the immediate people, on to the nations:

> *"Thus says the LORD, the Redeemer of Israel and his Holy One,*
> *to one deeply despised, abhorred by the nation, the servant*
> *of rulers: 'Kings shall see and arise; princes, and they shall*
> *prostrate themselves; because of the LORD, who is faithful,*
> *the Holy One of Israel, who has chosen you'"* (Isaiah 49:7).

The New Testament scriptures pick up this theme of Messianic chosen-ness and the implication for the nations:

> *And a voice came out of the cloud, saying, "This is my Son, my*
> *Chosen One; listen to him!"* (Luke 9:35).

> *"Behold, my servant whom I have chosen, my beloved with whom*
> *my soul is well pleased. I will put my Spirit upon him, and*
> *he will proclaim justice to the Gentiles"* (Matthew 12:18).

Jesus does not tell a new story but a new chapter in the continuing story. However, his chapter is clearly the one that changes the entire story. He referenced himself as the fulfillment of the Scriptures—the Holy Book (Mark 14:49). He was the climax to what had been long anticipated in the story of a people chosen for a purpose. His chosen-ness as prophet, priest, and king does not lead him to positions of privilege but to places of servitude. This is expressed in the language of the Philippians hymn (Philippians 2:6-11): he did not grasp his place in eternal power, he emptied himself, taking the form of a servant; he humbled himself so much as to accept death on a cross. His chosen role was all directed to blessing others, even unto the nations (Matthew 28:18-20; Acts 1:8).

As Jesus was chosen to be God's agent, so Jesus chose his followers out of the divine initiative of love.

> *"You did not choose me, but I chose you and appointed you that you should go and bear fruit and that your fruit should abide, so that whatever you ask the Father in my name, he may give it to you"* (John 15:16).

This new group of people, a branch of the original, is a group "chosen by grace" (Romans 11:5). Again, the choosing was not because of the specialness inherent in the chosen ones but in the nature of the One choosing. "God chose what is foolish in the world to shame the wise..." (I Corinthians 1:27). The story always begins with God, and God sustains the ongoing plot as well.

The make-up of the people of God (Ephesians 1:4; I Thessalonians 1:4) now shifts from one ethnic group to many "nations" (again the Greek sense of εθνοσ) united in a common identity of adoption into the God-family through redemption and adoption in Jesus. The holy nation becomes composed of many nations (I Peter 2:9). Again, their chosen-ness is not as much privilege as it is to sacrifice, serve, and even suffer with

Christ for the sake of all nation-families coming back into vibrant relationship with God, their heavenly Father (I Peter 2:12; 4:12-14).

What was made clear for the community was also expressed to individuals. The Lord visited Ananias with a message regarding the rescue of the terrorist and murderer Saul (Paul),

> But the Lord said to him, "Go, for he is a chosen instrument of mine to carry my name before the Gentiles and kings and the children of Israel" (Acts 9:15).

The aspects of chosen-ness immediately come to our attention in this verse. Saul was selected not because of anything inherent in himself—he was an enemy of God's new nation or branch of people. And chosen-ness came with the intention of agency—Saul would become Paul, the great missionary to the nations.

Chosen-ness—the inexplicably great privilege of being rescued. Chosen-ness—the resulting great responsibility of engaging in the Restoration Project.

12

CHOSEN TO BE A BLESSING: HISTORICAL NARRATIVE OF CHOSEN-NESS AS RESPONSIBILITY

WHEN FOLLOWING THE HISTORY OF THE CHURCH from the beginning of the New Testament through to the present, we see, down through each epoch or chapter of the story, the same struggle of crossing boundaries. There seems to be a natural dynamic that happens within the family as it struggles to find its new identity: a forming of exclusive, tight boundaries. In some ways, this dynamic is to be expected. It is a natural reflex to spend one's time and resources in caring for one's immediate family. Additionally, there is danger outside the family, and so the members bind together in familiarity and safety.

Over time, though, this sense of security becomes a barrier preventing the family members from fulfilling their chosen responsibility to reach out and invite in new family members. It takes a radical group of family members to push the idea that the family does not exist primarily for itself. It takes a prophetic voice to call the rest of the family to a decision to reach beyond its boundaries to enlarge the family. This voice calls them to move beyond that first-level decision, when they became a part of the family of God. It invites them to make a second-level decision to become proactive in inviting others into the family. Historically, the church has struggled with this tension of hoarding or protecting the blessing, and with the call to take the blessing out to those outside the family.

Consider the following examples from the historical expansion of the church, examples of those who made this second-level decision and accepted the calling to cross boundaries.

The first apostles set the tone. The Acts of the Apostles documents the journey of Philip to the outpost of Samaria and to a special assignment of witness to an Ethiopian ruler (Acts 8). Tradition also notes that he preached in Phrygia (west central Turkey). Tradition holds that Thomas left the comforts of Jerusalem and the safe family to bring the gospel to India. James chose not to remain in the holy city of Jerusalem but ventured out as a missionary to Spain. Nathanael is credited with preaching in Egypt, Arabia, Ethiopia, and Persia. Ten of the original twelve apostles served as active witnesses, ending in the ultimate witness as martyrs for the faith. Only John lived a long life, and a portion of that was in Asia Minor and as a banished fugitive for the faith on the Island of Patmos. The clear point is made by the circumstances of their lives and their ultimate deaths: chosen-ness is not for privileged position on earth but for a life of responsibility in the Restoration Project as God's agent of rescue.

There is an interesting connection to this notion of witness as *martyr* in the Greek language. The word *witness, martureo* (μάρτυρεω), is where we get our word *martyr* in English. Witness to Christ has always come with a cost. The earliest apostles gave ultimate testimony to the reality of God's love in Jesus by giving up all to follow him, and then crossing boundaries to give even their lives for the sake of that witness. This path was so common that the writer of Hebrews encourages those running their race to not lose courage because they "had not resisted to the point of shedding blood" (Hebrews 12:4). Though most of us are not called to be martyrs in the literal sense, we are all called to be martyrs in the witness sense. It is in this place of witness that we most clearly partner with God in his work. Jesus said that the work of the Spirit was to "bear witness about me," and the work of his followers was also to "bear witness" (John 15:26-27). In fact, bearing witness was to be the result of Holy Spirit empowerment on the newly formed church, as they were mandated by Jesus to be "witnesses to…the ends of the earth" once they had been so empowered (Acts 1:8).

The Restoration Project has been in play throughout history. However, it has seemed to move in fits and bursts only as individuals call the group to not lose sight of their responsibility of chosen-ness. Every so often, someone within the groups raises his eyes out beyond the safety of the group to see the world outside. That individual or smaller group calls the larger group to live beyond its natural boundaries and family lines.

Four hundred years later, St. Patrick became a missionary right out of the biblical model. Initially, this young man of privilege was captured from Gaul and carried to Ireland as a slave. As a slave he developed a vibrant relationship with God and, through his role as a herder for his slave owner, he learned to hear God through natural revelation and trust him in the face of the ruggedness and uncertainty of the elements. His cultural Christian experience from Gaul was transformed into a vibrant relationship in his setting of suffering and lost privilege. One day, as a slave, he heard God declare to him to go to the coast because his liberators would be found off shore in a passing vessel. He obeyed and he was rescued and taken back to Gaul.

His life had been so transformed by the slave experience that he prepared for vocational service for God. With the best training he was groomed to be a leader among his own people. But he could not escape the sense that he had been chosen into the Restoration Project, not to simply hoard the Rescue blessing. We see throughout history that spiritual renewal is often accompanied by a greater commitment to God's mission to reach his lost family. Patrick returned to his former slave masters to bring them spiritual liberation. Certainly, that took him outside the comfortable and safe circle of his chosen family.

When hearing the story of Patrick, one cannot help but see the connections to multiple biblical stories. He was taken into slavery, a slavery that eventually led to the saving of many (Joseph). He learned the inside of a culture by being planted there, which then set him up perfectly to be an ambassador across boundaries back into that culture (Moses, Saul). He made sacrifices of comfort to go back to his oppressive enemy (Jonah). He became the announcer and demonstrator of a better way rooted in the Kingdom of God (Jesus). This is the biblical story being retold in history. And notice, the institutional church was not fully on board with the retelling of the larger story. Church leadership tried to stop him from returning to the land of his slavery. It took a second-level decision by one of the chosen ones to lead the way.

Today, Patrick is known as the patron saint of Ireland. Interestingly, he was not Irish but a boundary crosser to the nations. He fulfilled the full plan of chosen-ness.

Then, down through the corridors of history, we find recorded the names of people who similarly took Jesus at his word. But it was not always a natural reflex. Thus, there are long periods when the church remains local and does not move out in search of the displaced families of God. Another great movement of purposeful going, though, is found in what is called the modern missionary movement. Many names in this movement have been recorded for us due to the advent of the printing press and the facility of preserving their stories.

Zinzendorf and the Moravians purposefully developed and deployed kingdom communities to live among those who had not yet experienced the King. Hudson Taylor, Adoniram Judson, and William Carey all stood up to the insular thinking of a well-formed European and American church; they dared to cross boundaries into Asia as ambassadors of God's love. David Livingston became the exploring missionary to Africa.

Another missionary to Africa, C.T. Studd, though much later historically than these modern-day pioneers, captured well this second-level calling to cross safe boundaries to seek dispersed family members. He declared, "some want to live within the sound of church or chapel bell; I want to run a rescue shop within a yard of hell."

Many others understood this chosen responsibility. These few examples only represent a few well-known examples from the Western-European-North American church. Since men wrote most of history of the Western church, often women or people of color are not always recorded in the story. However, there were many who were key to the movement even though their stories are not told as prominently.

Mary Slessor was one of the women whose story found its way into print. She has been called the dauntless Scottish lass of Nigeria. When she arrived in West Africa, she found a missionary community living in a European bubble of Victorian ghetto lifestyle. As the Eternal Son had, she emptied herself of privilege: she took on a lifestyle of incarnation among the people she wanted to experience the love of the Father. She was a trailblazer into areas where other missionaries were unwilling to go and to areas where some who did go willingly did not survive. Ruther Tucker has an excellent book that celebrates the many stories of women who were used by God to cross boundaries with the gospel.[1]

Behind all these stories of missionaries going are the lives of the people of the nations who received the message of invitation back into the family of God. Their stories too often go unrecorded. They truly knew what it meant to take up their cross and follow Jesus. Many were chased from families, lost work, were persecuted in a Pauline missionary fashion, and even themselves became martyrs for their new faith. In Mali, I became aware of many of these stories.

Bakari Saba, from the Boso fishermen tribe, heard the good news and came into relationship with God through Jesus. He was rejected by his family and people, yet today there are very few from the Boso people who are fully reunited to their Creator through Jesus. Bakari became a fisher of men and a boundary-crosser: he traveled with expatriate missionaries in the reaching of other tribal groups (nations) in Mali.

Belecko, a Fulani convert, was stoned by the people of his village and chased from his family. As an itinerate evangelist, he also became witness to the other tribes of Mali. God used him as an ambassador in several people's movements that led to thousands in Mali being restored fully into God's family.

Bakari and Blecko represent scores of untold stories of people who understood that they had been chosen with a renewed purposefulness in the Restoration Project.

Even though much of the second wave of mission is referred to as the Modern missionary movement, there is a more recent movement. Perhaps, in scope, it is the greatest missions movement of history. Since 1960, the people of the southern hemisphere and those of the Asian churches have been part of the largest burst of Christian faith in history, as missionaries are now regularly sent from places such as Korea, Nigeria, China, Brazil, and the Philippines. Many of these areas are referred to as the majority world.

Those who were invited into the family of God through Jesus Christ and through the missionary mechanism, refused to remain as solely missionary-receiving churches, but took on the calling to be sending churches. They were missionaries at the core; they made sacrifices to cross boundaries, recognizing chosen-ness to be as much a responsibility as it is a privilege.

Today we celebrate them as strategically placed agents of God in his plan to love the world.

More recently, through globalization, we are observing an unparalleled movement of people in history. This global dynamic has created another missions movement—the diaspora on mission with God. Many of these mobile people did not set out in spiritual pursuit or with a spiritual intention as proactive missionaries. However, in search of a better life materially, many of this diaspora have found full reunion with the God family through Jesus. Others have been witness to their standing of hope in that family as they have shared the good news of Jesus in their movements.

In this section on the movements of missions through the centuries since Christ first sent his chosen ones, I have chosen some big names to highlight. Several represent turning points and what might be called moments of rediscovery of a complete theology of chosen-ness unto the Restoration Project. As a result of the brevity of my recounting, many stories go untold. Some were local and some were global. Some involved the sacrifice of going and others the sacrifice of sending. Some were great adventures, while others were sustained obedience in the daily ordinariness of most of our lives. Regardless of whether told or not, each story has somehow been grafted onto God's larger story. Those who have been more proactive and intentional in co-telling with God have found a great sense of restored purpose in life as children of the Rescue.

TODAY

Today's people of God are still faced with the same question: What will we do with our chosen-ness? The same principles at work in the Israel story, in the early church story, and down through history, are still at play in our story. God is still intent on declaring his love to the nations and on drawing them back into vibrant relationship. He chooses his people to be engaged in that movement. We will either cooperate with God in proactive partnership or he will help move us. God is committed to this story line, to completing his Big Story. The final declaration of Scripture, the Apocalypse of John, is a deposit on his commitment to bring it to fruition.

We are Chosen! But not chosen just to privately enjoy God's favor! We are chosen to be employed in the Restoration Project. Sought after to become a seeker. We are receivers of the Sent One to become one of the sent ones. We are invited into the Restoration Project through being rescued. We either go as active agents or we go kicking and screaming. The first way is a lot more fulfilling! But with either, God's heart-passion is fulfilled.

GOD loves you. You are special. But you are not the end all of his love. You are chosen to live in a way that declares that everyone else is worthy of his love as well. The next step in being intentional in our chosen-ness responsibility is to explore our unique calling and calling assignments in this amazing story.

PART III

RESCUED FOR THE RESTORATION PROJECT: CALLED TO A SPECIFIC ASPECT OF THE RESTORATION PROJECT

FILMS HAVE A WAY OF OPENING UP our divine imagination. Our favorite films, the ones that inspire us, often echo the larger story that God is telling. The idea of destiny or calling is one of the classic movie themes, and *Chariots of Fire* is one example of a movie with this theme. The film tells the story of Eric Liddell, an Olympic track medalist, but the movie tells a much deeper story than that of Liddell's athletic accomplishments. It tells the story of a man who lived by principle, trusting God to make him successful in accordance with God's definition of success. As Eric lived in active partnership with God he became more aware of his calling.

In the course of the film, we learn that Eric is preparing to follow a calling to be a missionary in China. His sister, though, is concerned that Eric's pursuit of gold medals in running will distract him from that calling. Eric assures his sister that nothing can keep him from obeying the call to follow God to China. He then delivers that well-known line: "I believe God made me for a purpose, but he also made me fast. And when I run, I feel his pleasure." When we discover our calling, we come alive. We move from merely existing to truly LIVING!

Eric Liddell understood calling on multiple levels. He lived out a daily relationship with God that made all of life worship. He also found his places of unique calling and contribution in God's Restoration Project. Once we discover that our chosen-ness is a gift to be used for others, we then can ask the questions surrounding the specific aspects of our life purpose. The next few chapters will unpack this notion of calling.

Chapter 13 will describe the nature of calling, while chapters 14–19 will offer biblical examples of how people found their calling in life. I have discovered six different categories of calling in my reading of Scripture. God works in many ways to reveal His calling to us. The biblical text is his most consistent source of revelation. As we consider these inspired accounts of specific callings found in God's Word, we can gain new perspectives on our own stories and how they fit in with the Larger Story that God is telling. Chapter 20 will complete this section of the book by offering some suggested next steps to find our calling or to reaffirm the calling we already know and to fully live out of that calling.

13

CALLING: FINDING OUR UNIQUE PLACE IN THE RESTORATION PROJECT

CALLING IS SIMPLY A DIVINE SUMMONS. It is the invitation from God to see our lives in light of the larger story that he is telling. Every person rescued by Jesus is called to play a role in the Restoration Project. In his book *The Call*, Os Guinness describes our need for calling, for purpose:

> "Deep in our hearts, we all want to find and fulfill a purpose bigger than ourselves. Only such a larger purpose can inspire

us to heights we know we could never reach on our own. For each of us the real purpose is personal and passionate: to know what we are here to do, and why."[1]

In *The Call*, Guinness reminds us that calling is first and foremost to someone (God) and not to something (business, politics, teaching, caring for the poor) nor to somewhere (Mongolia, the inner city, Ohio). The *what* and the *where* of our calling will later become important as God guides us into our specific assignments. Before we seek the *what* and the *where*, though, we must first understand the *who*. God's invitation back into relationship is far weightier than his calling us to a given task. We are chosen to be sons and daughters of God before we are called to be servants of God—**relationship before program!** The person I am and am becoming is far more important to God than the contribution I make. But who I am and what I am called to do often move in tandem.

The Bible suggests that God has assignments for us that might be described as a "calling," the natural overflow of our relationship with him. Many factors impact that sense of calling. God has created each person uniquely—we are fearfully and wonderfully made (Psalm 139:14). The process of our redemptive stories is filled with unique twists and turns that play out in our realized calling. Nothing gets wasted in the economy of God. Then in Christ we are given Holy Spirit empowered grace-gifts that flow through that calling. Each person has a unique role and unique assignments in the larger story that God is telling. This is calling!

Once we acknowledge that we are called, then the task, the place, and the method for living out that unique calling follow in the form of guidance from God. When thinking of specific examples of calling, people often point to Paul's "Macedonian Call" (Acts 16:9-10). Paul's calling, however, came to him years earlier. When the Macedonian man appeared to him in a vision, Paul was simply receiving guidance for his next assignment in the Restoration Project. At that moment of his life he was already living out his relationship with God and faithfully fulfilling what he knew of his calling. In the flow of that day-to-day, he became aware of the next *where* of that calling.

How do we find our unique calling? Some people become paralyzed, unable to live out their faith, because they believe they must wait for a lightning bolt to hit them with God's calling. But God tends to work in multiple ways, not just in lightning bolts. Taking a deeper look at calling may help us eliminate some misconceptions about it and may help us recognize God's call for us. With this understanding we will then be able to respond to God's initiative in our lives in the same way that several people in the Scriptures did: "Here am I, send me!" I like to begin with a distinction between general and specific calling.

GENERAL CALLING

"General calling" is a sense that our lives belong to God; as a result, we live with a clear sense of the need to steward the resources that he has given us: time, talent, treasure, the gospel—our very lives themselves. In this sense, all of life becomes the believer's calling. Os Guinness clearly describes this embrace:

> "Calling is the truth that God calls us to himself so decisively that everything we are, everything we do, and everything we have is invested with a special devotion and dynamism and direction lived out as a response to his summons and service."[2]

With this perspective, each breath, each moment, day in and day out, life itself, becomes worship. Everything becomes a reflection of the divine initiative in our lives and an opportunity to reflect his glory.

This idea of worship is captured in the Holy Spirit's exhortation through Paul to the faithful in the church in Rome: "present your bodies as a living sacrifice" (Romans 12:1). We generally think of that exhortation in its implication to holiness, but there is a deeper reality embedded in the notion of sacrifice. Sacrifice is worship language. Our first calling is to worship God through every aspect of our lives. I think the definition of worship given by William Temple, Archbishop of Canterbury, captures this general sense of calling in our response to the summons of God.[3]

> *Worship is the submission of all our nature to God.*
> *It is the quickening of conscience by His holiness;*
> *the nourishment of mind with His truth;*
> *the purifying of imagination by His beauty;*
> *the opening of heart to His love;*
> *the surrender of will to His purpose –*
> *and all of this gathered up in adoration,*
> *the most selfless emotion of which our nature is capable*
> *and therefore the chief remedy for that self-centeredness*
> *which is our original sin and the source of all actual sin.*

The Apostle Paul summarizes this type of God-initiated, God-focused, and God-glorifying life with the following exhortations:

*"And **whatever** you do, in word or deed, do everything in the name of the Lord Jesus, giving thanks to God the Father through him"* (Colossians 3:17).

*"**Whatever** you do, work heartily, as for the Lord and not for men"* (Colossians 3: 23).

By using "whatever," Paul shows that everything of life, both great and small, can be consecrated to God's glory. When we live this way, we are living out the Great Commandment, loving God with all our being. And when we love God with all of our being, there is an immediate sense of the need to love our neighbor as our self. This is the general calling for each of us who has been rescued.

When we make these realities our everyday philosophy, we do not need to spend long hours worrying about whether we might be missing our calling. We realize that "we are God's handiwork, created in Christ Jesus to do good works, which God prepared in advance for us to do" (Ephesians 2:10). In that space of living out what we already know of God's will, we can pray for and be alert to specific divine assignments that come our way. If we are loving God with all our being, over time his heart desires will become our heart desires. Then the flow of our lives will become an ongoing expression of his life in and through us. When we are loving God with all our being, we can live the life described by St. Augustine: "Love God with all your heart and do what you like."

SPECIFIC CALLING

However, as we become more aware of a specific calling, or

specific callings in our life, we can maximize our stewardship of time, talent, treasure, and the gospel itself, in the direction of the specific calling. Our specific calling consists of the tasks, roles, or assignments uniquely commissioned to us by God whereby we fulfill his will in a given time, space, and manner. Sometimes this calling comes through a direct, specific, or supernatural communication from God.

At other times, our specific calling is realized while we are in the process of fulfilling our ordinary calling, simply fulfilling our responsibilities of life. We serve our families, our churches, and our communities, all by the power of the Holy Spirit. Then one day we look back on our lives and we see that our specific calling was being worked out through simple faithfulness to what was already clearly shown to us. Slowly, convictions and practices meld into a calling.

For others, a calling in life develops through what Bill Hybels calls "a holy discontent."[4] We see something broken in our world and find we can no longer ignore it, and so we commit time and resources to address the problem. The holy discontent becomes a specific calling as we commit to become part of God's solution of repair and restoration.

Some of the other names we use to refer to a more focused life are vocation, ministry, life purpose, vision, mission, or even avocation. John Eldredge describes the moment of realizing one's purpose, mission, or calling in the following way: "Something in your heart says, 'Finally—it has come. This is what I was made for.'"[5] Sometimes our calling is not just one *aha* moment, as Eldredge describes, but several moments of realizing that we have been prepared for different assignments along the journey of life. This is where we see the close relation of calling, mission, or life purpose.

Sometimes these assignments are revealed in stages, as building blocks to a larger mission or more precise calling. In the leadership language of Bobby Clinton, he refers to moments of life convergence, where we realize new places or levels of calling.

> "Convergence takes place in a leader's life when giftedness, role, and influence come into alignment with experience, personality, formation, opportunity, and destiny."[6]

Life is great when we arrive at those *aha* moments of life purpose, mission, or calling. But the truth of the matter is that we rarely just arrive at a sense of specific calling. It usually comes through theological reflection on our lives and the story that God has been telling in, around, and through our life experiences.

We will move to some biblical examples of calling to allow our minds to enter into sanctified reflection on what our own calling might be. Eugene Peterson writes, "Story incites story. Storytellers swap stories."[7] We began our search for the purpose of life in the narrative of Jonah. We now will allow other biblical characters to speak into our calling imaginations.

14

CHILDHOOD CALLING

A CHILDHOOD CALLING can be characterized as a revealed calling from the Lord given to a child or young person early in life. That calling may come either directly from God to the person, or it may come to that person through his or her family, or the calling may simply be given to the family. This type of calling is embraced at an early age even though the realization or launch of that calling might not come to complete fruition until much later in life.

JOSEPH

The first example of childhood calling that comes to mind from the Scriptures is found in the life of Joseph, as told in Genesis. Joseph's calling began with two dreams of destiny. Because Joseph was his father's favorite son, Joseph's brothers were already jealous of him. When he shared with them his dreams of them bowing down to him, the brothers were driven from attitudes of jealousy to actions rooted in hate. In a state of jealousy, they sold Joseph into slavery, and he was later trafficked in Egypt. Eventually, through a series of amazing circumstances, Joseph's destiny, as foretold in his dream, was manifested: his brothers did bow down to him—three times before discovering his identity and then once again after the death of their father Jacob (Israel). Joseph's dream was fulfilled fourfold.

God had a calling for Joseph, a task that was more for the preservation of the people of God than for the sake of that Gentile nation. Joseph went involuntarily to that Gentile nation; still, he lived as a reflection of God's glory. Throughout Joseph's story his captors recognized God's favor in his life. Pharaoh declared, "Can we find a man like this, in whom is the Spirit of God?" (Genesis 41:38). And by the end of the story, Joseph understood how his destiny had come to fruition, even if through an indirect route:

> *"As for you, you meant evil against me, but God meant it for good, to bring it about that many people should be kept alive, as they are today"* (Genesis 50:20).

What is important in Joseph's story is that there were many times when it seemed that his destiny would not be fulfilled.

He faced many setbacks, but he never gave up, and the favor of God never departed from him. If we base the unfolding of our calling only by what seems obvious, we might miss the subtext that God is telling behind the scenes. Given the visible circumstances, it would have been easy for Joseph to miss the subtext of God's Bigger Story, and to assign the early dreams to bad lamb and couscous eaten the night before.

In such an instance, and given his circumstances, Joseph might also have been tempted to abandon God's way altogether, but we observe him living in integrity throughout his life. It was in faithfulness to the daily walk with God that he never lost his favor. There is a principle embedded in this lesson of the story: **Do not abandon too early a calling, a prophetic word, or a vision that God has revealed!**

SAMUEL

Another example of a childhood calling is that of the prophet Samuel (I Samuel). He was a miracle baby, born to a barren mother. His mother, Hannah, had cried out to the Lord for a child, and the Lord heard her cry. When God blessed her with this new life, she had an immediate sense of stewardship of the child. He belonged to God and she was merely the steward of God's gift, acting as his caretaker. Even though Samuel was her only child, she consecrated him to the Lord.

> "*As soon as the child is weaned, I will bring him, so that he may appear in the presence of the Lord and dwell there forever*" (I Samuel 1:22).

Her husband, Elkanah, agreed with her, and so she brought Samuel to the Temple to serve under Eli. She declared unequivocally that Samuel belonged to the Lord (I Samuel 1:28).

We do not know what Hannah and Elkanah heard from the Lord that brought them to this decision, but they recognized a calling for their son to serve the priest. Even though he was their miracle son, they could not keep him. The Lord blessed their sacrifice—not only in terms of the greater story of the people of God but also through personal fruitfulness. Hannah and Elkanah were blessed with other children to steward for God: three more sons and two daughters.

It was while Samuel was faithfully serving Eli the priest that he received his specific calling. We might say that he was living out his general calling as a servant of God, and while he was faithfully doing this, his specific calling to be a prophet began to take form. It started with an audible call in the night. Samuel heard his name. After he approached Eli several times, the older priest recognized that God was calling Samuel. Eli told Samuel to return to his room and, the next time the Lord called, to answer, "Speak, Lord, your servant hears" (I Samuel 3:9). The next call came with a sense of urgency, "Samuel! Samuel!" but this time Samuel was ready.

This was the beginning of his prophetic calling. It was also a fresh chapter in revelation of God for the people. I Samuel 3:1 notes that, "in those days the word of the LORD was rare; there were not many visions." Thereafter, Samuel received messages from God, some challenging and some promising. As he proved faithful in delivering both types of messages, the Lord increased the flow of the messages. "And Samuel grew, and the Lord was with him and let none of his words fall to the ground"

(I Samuel 3:19). Samuel became established as a prophet of the Lord (I Samuel 3:20).

Samuel's realization of his calling began with his parents, and was fostered by a discerning priest. It was delivered by an audible voice. Samuel walked into that calling through faithfulness to what others had shown him and in obedience to God's direct revelation. There is a lesson of process hidden in Samuel's calling. Sometimes we spend a period of time faithfully serving in a mundane role—Samuel as servant to Eli the priest—and in that period of faithful service God is grooming us for our ultimate calling. I call this *the Samuel principle*: **Be faithful in the small things and at the right time God will release the larger assignments.**

DAVID

A third story of a childhood or youth destiny calling is that of David. The story is riddled with suspense. Israel's first king, Saul, had proved to be a poor ruler and an ungodly leader. Samuel even mourned his part in calling Saul to be king, but the Lord told Samuel to move on from his grieving and to go to the family of Jesse, since one of Jesse's sons would be the new king. The sons were paraded before the prophet. When Samuel saw Eliab, the oldest son, he thought, "Surely the Lord's anointed is before him" (I Samuel 16:6). His estimation came from Eliab's appearance and stature. But the Lord rebuked Samuel, and we learn that "the Lord sees not as man sees; man looks on the outward appearance, but the Lord looks on the heart" (I Samuel 16:7).

Eventually Samuel saw all of Jesse's sons that had been brought before him, but received no confirmation from the

Lord. Then the youngest son was called from the field to come before Samuel. And the Lord said to Samuel, "Arise and anoint him, for this is he" (I Samuel 16:12). As Samuel anointed David, the Spirit of the Lord rushed upon David. David's calling from the Lord was confirmed through prophetic recognition and Holy Spirit demonstration.

God's call came to David when he was still young. It was delivered to him through Samuel, a man of God. It is important to remember, though, that over twenty years passed from this moment of anointing until David actually took the royal throne. Over eighteen of those years he spent in the wilderness, *En Gedi*, being chased by the jealous king Saul. We see again a feature common in the lives of God's called servants: **there is often a lag between the time of calling and its realization.**

JESUS

Jesus's calling is an obvious example of childhood destiny calling. Sometime we have a hard time thinking of Jesus in his humanity. But he too grew into his calling. It was revealed to his earthly father and mother, first through the declaration of angels. Then the calling was confirmed with an amazing account of revelation prior to his birth: the response of John Baptist while still in Elizabeth's womb. After his birth, Jesus's calling was confirmed by angels to shepherds, by the prophetess Anna and the prophet Simeon when Mary and Joseph had Jesus circumcised, and by journeying magi who came from afar. Mary pondered each of these confirmations. Even with all of these signs, Mary had to grow into an understanding of the full meaning of Jesus's calling.

We do not know when Jesus became fully aware of this destiny. He hinted at an awareness of it when he was left in the

Temple at the age of twelve (Luke 2:41-51). However, it appears that a full awareness of that calling took time to develop, even for Jesus. Luke indicates that Jesus grew into his calling—"And Jesus increased in wisdom and in stature and in favor with God and man"—and his public ministry was not inaugurated until his baptism eighteen years after this event (Luke 3:21-23).

One last word on childhood calling: **We all are created with destiny; thus, in one sense, everyone has a destiny from childhood**. Our lives are rich with purpose right from the beginning. Some of us know early, or at least our families know early, our assignment(s) in the unfolding of our destinies. The context of our families and the spiritual perception of our adult caretakers can have an impact in realizing that calling. Joseph's family was not ready for his dream and so jealousy took over. Samuel's parents prepared well the way for him to experience his calling. David's family was surprised that the youngest would be king—they were stuck with some cultural blinders on and David's brothers mocked him when he showed up on the battlefield as Goliath was taunting Israel. Even Jesus's family had a hard time getting their minds completely around his calling and identity as the Messiah.

There are some lessons here for those of us who are stewarding children as gifts from God. We should be careful not to block our children out from an ultimate life calling by shaping them for lesser pursuits—gaining wealth, having a comfortable or prestigious life, being served rather than serving. I once heard a mission leader say that the need for missionaries was not a result of kids not wanting to make a difference but of parents steering their kids away from the possibility. We need to give imagination to potential callings of radical service for the greatest treasure that we steward—our children and grandchildren.

Most of us, however, do not have the privilege of knowing our destiny or calling in childhood. As we will see in the next types of calling, many of us only become aware of our calling later, as adults. This realization invites each of us to enter into a process of discernment to better understand our calling. We will explore this more after all of the types of calling have been unfolded.

15

MIDLIFE CALLING AND LIFE SHIFT

A MIDLIFE SHIFT COULD BE DESCRIBED as a life change with purpose. It is often expressed in terms of a vocation, but it could also be avocational or bi-vocational. Sometimes this calling is delivered through one of God's servants—human or angelic. Sometimes the revelation of this new calling comes directly from God and then is confirmed by the faith community. This seems to be the most common calling in the Scriptures.

ABRAM-ABRAHAM

Abram had a midlife call. We know nothing of Abram's

background except that his father, Terah, served other gods than Yahweh (Joshua 24:2) and that he was living in Haran with his family. We have no clues that Abram was pursuing the Living God, and so God's calling comes without explanation: "Now the Lord said to Abram, 'Go from your country…to the land I will show you" (Genesis 12:1). Although Abram did not realize it at the time, this call from God was setting him out on journey to become the father of faith. This new calling would bestow him with a new name, Abraham, and would launch him on his journey with a new covenant, founded on God's promises. The end result was the establishment of a new chapter, not just in Abraham's story, but also in the Bigger Story that God was telling.

GIDEON

Gideon had a similar experience of calling, but his did not come via a human agent; an angel delivered it. During Gideon's lifetime, the people of God were being harassed by other nations. The Midianites and the Amalekites would raid and plunder the Israelites' crops. Judges 6:6 states that "the people of Israel cried out to the LORD." In response, the Lord sent an angel to Gideon to call him to mobilize the people of Israel in taking a stand. The angel found Gideon beating out wheat in the winepress, an unusual place to perform a task that was usually done outside. Gideon was there, though, to hide from the Midianites.

The angel of the Lord appeared to Gideon and said,

> "*The LORD is with you, O mighty man of valor… Go in this might of yours and save Israel from the hand of Midian; do not I send you?*" (Judges 6:12, 14).

Mighty man of valor? Gideon didn't look mighty when viewed through human eyes. Gideon himself questioned his ability to lead in such a task. In fact, many of God's servants throughout the centuries have felt woefully inadequate for the tasks assigned to them by God. They—and we—are correct: we *are* inadequate if we view ourselves and our situations through natural eyes, if we are considering only our own abilities. But each of these individuals was promised that God would go before them and that he would be the guarantor of success.

Gideon, though, did not overcome this natural fear very easily. He was looking too much at himself and too little at God. He apparently did not trust God's evaluation, and he wanted God to prove himself. Thus, he became the patron saint of "fleecing God." In doing so, he falls in the long line of servants of God who repeatedly questioned God. Their stories teach us about **God's faithfulness to fulfilling his calling in us in spite of our fears and weaknesses.**

ELISHA

Elisha is a good example of someone who experienced a midlife calling delivered through a prophet. His calling begins with a word from the Lord to the prophet Elijah: "And Elisha, the son of Shaphat of Abel-meholah, you shall anoint to be prophet in your place." (I Kings 19:16) Elijah found Elisha plowing with twelve yoke of oxen—evidence that, up to this point, Elisha's vocation, at least in part, had been farming. When he found Elisha, Elijah delivered God's call to Elisha by placing his cloak on Elisha (from which we get the symbol of the prophet's mantle). Elisha then went immediately to his parents to take leave of them. The complete shift from Elisha's past pursuit to his new calling was symbolized in the breaking up of the yokes to fuel a fire and the boiling of the oxen in a celebratory meal. "Then he rose and went after Elijah and assisted him" (I Kings 19:21).

After the calling came training. Elisha served as an apprentice of Elijah. Callings need to be developed. While walking alongside Elijah, Elisha came to realize the source of Elijah's success as a prophet: it was the Holy Spirit operating through him. Thus, before Elijah's departure, Elisha asked Elijah for a double portion of his spirit (II Kings 2). A spiritual endowment was transferred to the new prophet, and immediately those around him saw the manifestation of this prophetic spirit. This type of calling has elements similar to the sponsorship calling described below, but it begins with a declaration of the call and a definite demarcation between one's past life and one's new life purposefully lived in answer to the call.

JONAH

Sometimes one's calling comes through a revelation directly from God and leads to a midlife shift. Jonah is an obvious example of revelation and midlife shift. Since we have just taken a larger look at his story, we will not develop it much at this point. Though we know nothing of his life before his calling, we do know that the word of the Lord came directly to him and this changed his course of life.

THE TWELVE

The original twelve disciples are also clear examples of midlife shift. Jesus came to each of them when they were already settled into their lives. Some were fishermen, one was a tax collector, and for some we do not know their previous occupations. Yet

Jesus's call to each of them was simple: "Follow me!" (Mark 1:17). Jesus first called them into a relationship with himself (Mark 3:14). This is where all our callings start: in a relationship with Jesus. But Jesus was also calling them into a form of apprenticeship; they had to grow into that calling. As they walked with him, they learned about the Kingdom and about Kingdom ministry. From this apprenticeship, they were eventually sent out to do all the things that Jesus had been doing: preaching (announcing the Kingdom), healing the sick, and casting out demons (demonstrating the Kingdom). They slowly walked into their calling as Kingdom-of-God ambassadors.

It is hard to believe that when they were called the disciples knew all that they were signing up for. They began simply by following one whom they thought was an anointed prophet. Over time, they came to realize that he was the Messiah. With this realization came a deeper understanding of their calling: to carry the message of Jesus. Each of these disciples would die for reasons directly connected to this calling. Judas the traitor would take his own life after contemplating his disloyalty to the Savior. Another ten disciples would die as martyrs—tragic and gruesome deaths that they could have escaped by renouncing the Lord. Only John lived to old age, yet his life too was greatly altered: he was exiled to the island of Patmos.

What is important here is that answering their calling meant leaving their original professions. Now we know that Jesus was the God-man and so his authority to call is clear to us. However, it took a while for the disciples to discover the full nature of the one they began to recognize as the Messiah. We see that they were all confused after his crucifixion. Several went back to what knew: fishing. We realize the great faith steps that they took to walk into their destiny and calling.

Many callings start in this simple way. The "Follow me" of Jesus, though, includes a call to carry our cross (Matthew 16:24). Carrying our cross does not only symbolize dying a tragic death. It can involve unexpected turns in life, struggles, sacrifices—all are elements of carrying our cross. It is often only later in the journey that we realize the full implications of such a call. Through God's guidance, though, the call gradually takes form, and later we look back in amazement on how God maps out the subsequent journey.

SAUL-PAUL

The most radical life shift that we see in the Bible in someone's calling is that of the apostle Paul. In the Acts of the Apostles, we are introduced to him as Saul. We know that he was a leather worker, a vocational skill that he used later as a traveling, church-planting missionary. However, when we are introduced to Saul, we are told he was a Pharisee who had the task of eliminating the new movement called "the Way"—the followers of Jesus. In this capacity, he was involved in the martyrdom of Stephen and the resulting persecution of the church. As he traveled to Damascus to imprison the members of the Way in an attempt to obliterate the movement, Saul received his calling (Acts 9). His life took a 180° turn, from chief persecutor to chief promoter of the Christian faith.

Saul's initial calling was a combination call to relationship and to assignment. When the resurrected Jesus appeared to him and knocked him to the ground, Saul was stunned spiritually and blinded physically. He was led to Damascus, where he convalesced, remaining blind for three days. The Lord called another man, Ananias, to minister to the fallen Saul. Ananias received a vision to go to Saul and to lay hands on him and heal him (Acts 9:10). During this vision, the Lord told Ananias where to find Saul and told him that Saul too was simultaneously receiving a vision showing him that Ananias was on his way; Saul would be ready for his arrival. It was during the calling of Ananias that God revealed Saul's life calling:

> *"Go, for he is a chosen instrument of mine to carry my name before Gentilesand kings and the children of Israel. For I will show him how much he must suffer for the sake of my name"* (Acts 9:15-16).

Ananias went to Saul and laid hands on him, and Saul received his sight and the filling of the Holy Spirit. In the short span of three days, Saul was called to Someone—Jesus—and was given a new assignment for life—apostolic boundary-crosser for Jesus. The previous destroyer of the Way became the Way's greatest advocate through a revelation from the resurrected Christ and through the confirmation of another Christ-follower. This was a profound midlife shift in allegiance, vocation, and avocation.

There is an insightful side note in the Saul-to-Paul story. His calling brought suffering. Paul's career as a missionary proclaimer and demonstrator of Jesus took him into many unpleasant situations:

> *"Five times I received at the hands of the Jews the forty lashes less one. Three times I was beaten with rods. Once I was stoned. Three times I was shipwrecked; a night and a day I was adrift at sea; on frequent journeys, in danger from rivers,*

*danger from robbers, danger from my own people, danger
from Gentiles, danger in the city, danger in the wilderness,
danger at sea, danger from false brothers; in toil and hardship, through many a sleepless night, in hunger and thirst,
often without food, in cold and exposure. And, apart from
other things, there is the daily pressure on me of my anxiety
for all the churches"* (II Corinthians 11:24-28).

Paul could be described as the greatest missionary in the
history of the church. However, his calling was not to greatness.
Greatness happened over time in the raw obedience of day-to-
day engagement in his calling and in the endurance of a great
deal of suffering.

This is an important insight on calling. Many people say
they want a special calling from God. I often hear, *I want to do
something great for God!* Really? The servants of God highlighted
in these sections experienced as much or more grief and struggle
in their calling as they did pure fulfillment and delight. I doubt
that Moses ever had a really good week after abandoning the
wilderness to lead the people to the Promised Land. Moreover,
he did not even get to enter the Promised Land but only saw it at
a distance. As already noted, Joseph and David experienced trials
on the way to their destinies. Ten of the twelve original disciples
were martyred. Calling comes with a price and a sense of abandonment in God's Story. Responding to Gods' call is like strap-
ping ourselves to the mast of God's ship. God is steering the ship,
and responding to his call means going where he is going—to the
broken and marginalized of our world. **Calling is very costly!**

16

HOLY DISCONTENT AND TEMPORAL SHIFT

A CALLING THROUGH HOLY DISCONTENT begins with a God-given righteous indignation about something that is broken in our world. The indignation then moves to action that usually requires risk and sacrifice on the part of the one being called. Bill Hybels coined the phrase, using it as the title of one of his books entitled *Holy Discontent.*[1] In the two cases noted below, the life shift was not for the entire remaining life of the person called, but was a temporary life shift. In both situations, the holy discontent began with news that came from a trusted family member.

NEHEMIAH

The story of Nehemiah is a classic example of holy discontent. Nehemiah was an Israelite, one of God's people deported to Babylon. He held a respected position as cupbearer to King Artaxerxes in the Persian Empire, entrusted with testing the king's wine for quality and safety. One day he received an envoy from Jerusalem with the news that the remnant of his people who were left in Jerusalem were in great trouble because the walls of the city were broken down. Nehemiah was stricken by the news:

> *As soon as I heard these words I sat down and wept and mourned for days, and I continued fasting and praying before the God of heaven* (Nehemiah 1:4).

As Nehemiah prayed and fasted, God developed in him a holy discontent. Although what was happening to God's people was occurring at a distance and had no direct impact on Nehemiah, he felt a responsibility. His inner conviction led him to mobilize his influence and risk his position of privilege by approaching the king about rebuilding the wall of Jerusalem. Thus, Nehemiah was granted temporary leave, receiving both authorization and supplies from the king (Nehemiah 2).

We do not know exactly what happened to Nehemiah after the project was completed, the walls were dedicated, and the covenant was re-ratified. However, it seems likely that his mission had a time limit, given the agreement that he made with King Artaxerxes and the implication of the king's question regarding the time needed to finish the project:

"How long will you be gone, and when will you return?"

(Nehemiah 2:6). Some callings arising out of holy discontent are seasonal, completed when the broken aspect of our world is restored. Nehemiah's calling may have been of this type.

ESTHER

Esther's calling is an example of holy discontent that is initiated through the testimony or calling of a trusted advisor. Esther was one of the Jews deported to Persia. Despite the marginalized existence of her people, she had risen to prominence through winning a beauty contest. Thus, she became one of the many queens of King Xerxes and found herself in the royal palace of Persia.

A man named Haman became antagonistic to the Jewish exiles and offered money for their destruction. Esther's uncle Mordecai made her aware of the danger, passing on to her the news of the Jews' potential imminent destruction. Then Mordecai brought Esther into the story through the famous line "and who knows whether you have not come to the kingdom for such a time as this?" (Esther 4:14). Esther experienced a kind of holy discontent about the situation. Her response shows that she heard this challenge as not merely a call from her uncle but as a beckoning from heaven. She told Mordecai to gather the Jews in prayer and fasting to set the stage for a bold act. "Then I will go to the king, though it is against the law, and if I perish, I perish" (Esther 4:16). In the end, she spoke with the king, and Haman was exposed as a conniving and deceitful person. He ended up being hung on the gallows that he had prepared for Mordecai and others.

Like Nehemiah, Esther was moved in her heart to take action in a situation that might otherwise not have impacted her own life. She put herself in danger to alleviate danger for others. Both Nehemiah and Esther received a calling from God through a sense of holy discontent. This type of calling is important to emphasize because we sometimes assume that calling comes from a voice or a dramatic bright light and is a moment when heaven invades earth. But these stories show that many callings come through messages or news passed on to us by another person. Through God's work in our lives, the news becomes a personal and spiritual calling, driving us to God for success in responding to the need.

What is interesting about this type of temporal or seasonal shift that takes the form of a holy discontent calling is that we need to always be alert. We never know when God is preparing a break-in of his kingdom. **Our ongoing conversation with him out of our general calling is the context in which we realize these new chapters and assignments in our lives.**

17

HOLY DISCONTENT AND PERMANENT SHIFT

HOLY DISCONTENT CAN SOMETIMES BE DELAYED by life circumstances. The holy discontent may get forgotten or may just
simmer under the surface of a person's conscience or emotions
for a period of time. Then, out of the blue, a revelation may
come from God to reignite the passion to address the brokenness. In this chapter we will look as holy discontents that lead
to permanent changes of vocation or ministry in the lives of
God's children.

MOSES

Moses is an example of an initial holy discontent that led to a permanent life shift. Like Nehemiah and Esther, he was given a place of privilege that his people did not receive. The apostle Stephen referenced the privileged upbringing of Moses: "And Moses was instructed in all the wisdom of the Egyptians, and he was mighty in words and deeds" (Acts 7:22). In spite of this, Moses felt a connection with his people, the Hebrews. One day his discontent over the oppression of his blood-people became too much to endure and he struck an Egyptian foreman, killing him. Moses tried to cover up the death, but he was eventually exposed and fled from Egypt in fear (Exodus 2:15).

Moses spent the next forty years in the wilderness, living as a shepherd. We do not know if during this time Moses continued to think of his people. The passage of forty years has a way of making an initial commitment or sense of social responsibility fade into memory. One day, though, God showed up in a burning bush (Exodus 3) and called Moses. Exodus 3-4 is one of the great biblical conversations between God and an individual about calling. God was calling Moses to liberate his people.

After forty years, Moses's idealism and his discontent over the situation of his people had dissipated. He had many objections to God's calling for him but, with some bold manifestations, God demonstrated his intention to go with Moses. He also offered Moses a partner in his calling: his brother Aaron. With this knowledge that God was with him, Moses remained faithful to the calling, and the next forty years of his life were spent as prophetic liberator.

When we object to God's calling, as Moses did, God doesn't just go away and give the assignment to someone else. He meets us at our point of need. He showed Moses that he would go with him and give him everything he needed to accomplish the job, including giving him a partner in the mission, Aaron. **He will always give us everything we need to accomplish the tasks he calls us to.**

18

SUBTLE REALIZATION THROUGH SPONSORSHIP AND GOD CONFIRMATION

CALLING FOR SOME IS A MORE GRADUAL PROCESS. While serving under a leader, a person may come to learn aspects of leadership that prepare him or her for their next assignment. The calling at times becomes evident through the mentoring, coaching, and validation of a senior leader. If the senior leader is listening well to God, then God will add his confirmation to the called one, through revelation and/or success.

JOSHUA

Joshua is the most obvious narrative of a calling through sponsorship. He followed Moses as leader of the Hebrew people. His training came as he served under Moses and was mentored by him for forty years, beginning from when Joshua was just a youth (Numbers 11:28). Joshua served as a general in the Israelite army (Exodus 17). Within time, he was named as an assistant to Moses (Exodus 24:13), helping Moses at the tent of meeting. Basically, he learned leadership and faith through close proximity to his superior.

The faith in God that Joshua was learning from Moses is demonstrated in his interaction with the spies when they investigated the Promised Land (Numbers 13). Of the twelve spies, only Joshua and Caleb viewed the taking of the new land through eyes of faith. Both were clear-eyed about the challenges that faced the Hebrews, yet they exhorted the people not to lose hope because God was with them and had already promised the land to them. Their bold faith in those moments pointed to the growth of Joshua as a leader. It is important for a leader to develop such a faith because calling always comes with opposition. Joshua was able to overcome the opposition not because of some inherent quality of his own life, but through his vision of the character of God and his faith in God's ability to bring victory for the people, things he had learned from Moses's example.

Eventually God informed Moses that Joshua would be Moses's successor (Deuteronomy 3:28). During a great speech about taking the Promised Land (Deuteronomy 31), Moses informed the people of Israel that Joshua would be their new leader. The words of their great leader Moses became the official sponsorship of Joshua that the people needed to hear. What

Joshua had gained through mentoring over the past forty years was then mobilized through a transfer of leadership.

The confirmation of Joshua's calling by the Lord is found in Joshua 1. We often think of this as Joshua's calling passage, but really it is merely the confirmation of what had already been revealed through Moses. What is interesting is that the elements of that calling as seen here in this chapter all link back to the life of Moses. In verse 1, Joshua is introduced as Moses's assistant. In verse 5, the calling given comes to Joshua with the promise that the Lord would be with him just as he was with Moses (Joshua 1:5). Then the Lord charges Joshua to be strong and courageous, never turning from the word of God that Moses had commanded, to walk fully into success and prosperity. **Calling finds its fulfillment when the servant walks out his life journey in the principles of God's design**.

Joshua finished his life with a declaration of the reliability of finding life fulfillment by standing on the promises of God. His farewell speech to the people of God is a testimony that all of God's promises had come to fruition in his lifetime (Joshua 23:14-15). In fact, he repeats this conviction five times. The principle embedded in his testimony is that calling comes with challenges, but the long-term promise of fulfillment in God's time and in God's way will sustain the one who follows God's call.

JOHN MARK

The story of John Mark is another example of realized and preserved calling through sponsorship. His story is different from Joshua's in that his sponsors became divided regarding his ability to fulfill the call. Nevertheless, God worked in all those involved and, in the end, John Mark was able to fulfill God's call for him.

Although we do not know much about how he began his vocation of ministry, we do know that, together with Paul and Barnabas, he was a member of the first missionary team sent out by the church. He was a cousin of Barnabas (Colossians 4:10), so Barnabas may likely have played a role in John Mark's calling. We do know that, at a latter crucial moment, Barnabas did act as an advocate and sponsor of John Mark's calling.

During that first journey, something happened to make John Mark lose courage and abandon the missionary team. Paul was so disgusted with him that he did not want to take John Mark on the second missionary journey. This friction led to the separation of the dynamic team of Barnabas and Paul, as captured in Acts 15:39: "And there arose a sharp disagreement, so that they separated from each other. Barnabas took Mark with him and sailed away to Cyprus."

John Mark may have been tempted to abandon his calling because of Paul's initial assessment of him. But Barnabas stepped in and continued his sponsorship of John Mark. As Paul continued on to Syria and Cilicia with a new team, Barnabas took John Mark with him to Cyprus. Through Barnabas's sponsorship, John Mark's calling was preserved; he returned to the ministry. Because of Barnabas's work, eventually Paul's impression of John Mark changed. We see this change of attitude in Colossians 4:10, where Paul sends greetings to the church from John Mark and encourages the church to receive John Mark when he arrives. Later, near the end of his life, Paul calls for John Mark's assistance: "Get Mark and bring him with you, for he is very useful to me for the ministry" (II Timothy 4:11).

The lesson of John Mark's account is that our sense of God's calling needs to remain strong in spite of circumstances or failures that might challenge that sense of calling. God will often help us through these difficult times by graciously giving us a human sponsor to confirm our call. We also see that not every leader will affirm our calling. Paul was used to sponsor many other leaders into their calling for kingdom advancement: Silas, Timothy, Luke, Priscilla and Aquila, Epaphroditus, to name just a few. But initially he was not the best mentor for John Mark. Everyone needs to find their Barnabas in order to fully enter into his or her calling.

19

REALIZATION OF CALLING THROUGH YEARS OF FAITHFUL LIVING

SOMETIMES CALLING IS NEITHER REVEALED in such a mysterious fashion, nor so obvious to us. Not everyone will experience a calling like those that have been described above. Sometimes calling just unfolds in a life of faithfulness to what we already know as the right thing to do. Then, after a full life of faithful living before God, we look back and we see that he was leading the whole process by his faithful hand. Oswald Chambers expresses well this idea of God hidden in the backdrop of all callings:

> The realization of the call in a person's life may come like a clap of thunder or it may dawn gradually. But however quickly or slowly this awareness comes, it is always accompanied with an undercurrent of the supernatural.[1]

The gradual dawning is just as supernatural as the thunderclap. Sometimes when people have lived like this, by simply doing the right thing day after day and year after year, they are able to later look back over life and realize that they were living out a calling all along, even though they had not been totally aware of it at the time.

We do not get the opportunity to hear the how, what, when, or where of the calling of many of the people used by God in his larger story. Sometimes we are just introduced to them midstream. Elijah was considered one of the big three prophets of old, yet we have no information regarding his call to ministry. Daniel's calling appears to flow out of his choice for faithfulness to God's way in everyday life. Hebrews 11 is called the great chapter of faith. It rehearses great moments when people took risks of faith to play a significant role in the plot of God's larger story. Their calling was to endure without seeing the results of their labor. Twice the writer of Hebrews declares that they "did not receive what was promised" (vv. 13, 39). It appears that they were having faith for future generations who would realize those promises. The calling in these situations seems to be a calling to faithful living.

Many people in the Jesus story had this type of calling. They were not part of the Twelve, but they simply showed up doing the right thing. Joseph, the earthly father of Jesus, did the righteous thing by not divorcing his pregnant fiancée. Mary, his mother, endured ridicule for the sake of the call to be the bearer of the Messiah. Though they each received their callings through angelic messengers, the fulfillment of the call required simple raw surrender and obedience. After years of waiting for the kingdom to come, a prophet and a prophetess welcomed the newly dedicated baby Jesus as the savior of the world. God gave them the spiritual eyes to see beyond the natural. Mary Magdalene, a former prostitute, anointed Jesus with perfume, which Jesus identified as preparation for his burial. Her act was outrageous to some but she discerned this as God's assigned moment and method of action. While Jesus's apostles fled, a host of women lived faithfully, staying with Jesus right up to his crucifixion. These women were also the first to experience the mystery of resurrection. Each was called, but in a number of these instances, the called ones were simply doing the right thing, being faithful to what they knew of their general calling for life. Many people have realized calling in hindsight, as they looked back over the moments of faithful living.

20

CALLING: LIVING ON PURPOSE IN THE RESTORATION PROJECT

UNDERSTANDING THE MULTIPLE WAYS that God calls, as seen in these biblical accounts, might trigger something in us to better understand our own callings. Once calling comes into focus, it has the potential to liberate us to engage fully in a present passion or holy discontent, recognizing that this was God's calling in our life. These examples can also eliminate the fear and uncertainty that keep us from discovering and living out our calling. In moving forward, I want to address some misconceptions that I have heard about calling.

One impediment to our living out a calling is the feeling that we have to discover it by a certain age. For example, when our daughter was in her early twenties, she was trying to figure out her next vocational steps after university. She was anxious that she might miss God's call, and so, as she weighed her options, she found it hard to make a decision to move forward. Her heart was right—she wanted to live out Creator Design, but feeling that she had to know the entire itinerary of her life journey was keeping her from taking the first step. True, some people get a clear sense of calling early in life, but often people find their calling over time. Even the destiny callings highlighted from the Bible did not make sense to the individuals until later in their lives.

A second common misconception about calling is that God only has one path to get us into his story and if we miss it we are then consigned to an unfulfilled life. Most of the stories we just explored are examples of God "drawing straight with crooked lines." The best way to find our long-term calling is to be faithful with what we know about our lives and about God's will for us right now. When we are already being faithful, God has a way of finding us and getting us to his assigned places.

A third misconception about calling is that we may mistakenly believe that we need to wait for the spectacular or amazing calling. When I was helping my daughter think through calling, she blurted out that she wanted "to have the amazing life that her mother and I had experienced." In hindsight, we have had an amazing adventure in serving God. But we did not set out to have an amazing life.

In the beginning we followed my primary calling to the

ministry of the Word. Ingrid found vocation in teaching elementary children and avocation in the church, around my calling. Later we were both called vocationally to be missionaries in Mali. When we returned from Africa, our lives took an unexpected turn through some unexpected life circumstances. I became a professor to live out my calling by preparing others to do the work of the ministry. Subsequently, this was amplified again in my new calling assignment as a local parish pastor, with adjunct teaching responsibilities in various institutes around the world. During this time Ingrid had multiple vocational and developmental pursuits. She has now landed in her sweet spot of calling as a leadership coach and minister of inner healing. At each stage of the process, we had not moved forward with the plan of entering a spectacular experience; we had simply followed God's call based on what we knew at each chapter of the story. In hindsight, we have had an amazing experience, but while we were in the midst of things, there were many days when it did not seem so spectacular. In fact, there have been many downright mundane and painful days.

If at the beginning of my journey someone had told me the route I would take, I would have been shocked and maybe even a bit tired before even beginning. But, in hindsight, each chapter in my story was intrinsically important, and, at the same time, was laying the groundwork for the next chapter. Furthermore, all of the chapters of my story are woven into his story. Now *that* fact is what I find amazing.

One day I was having coffee with a friend who was sorting through some of his life experiences. He was living with some challenging situations resulting from bad choices and a broken marriage. But Jesus had rescued him, and now he wanted to have an amazing return in the second half of his life; he wanted to make an extraordinary contribution to life to make up for lost time and lost opportunities.

In frustration he asked, "What if I am called to just be ordinary?"

In truth, everyone is both ordinary and special at the same time. Even the biblical characters we hope to emulate were quite ordinary, but they had a God who does the extraordinary. Even Jesus, who does not fit at all in the ordinary category, still worked with simple things to accomplish the Father's mission: a human body, a backwater hometown, ordinary and even uninspiring followers, mud, spit, bread, water, and wine. In Jesus we see this mix of the ordinary and the extraordinary: a borrowed donkey for a triumphal entry, a borrowed tree for the making of a king, a borrowed tomb in which to prepare for spectacular resurrection.

My friend then added, "What if my role is not to be amazing but to connect others to amazing opportunities?" Wow!

My response: "That would be a well-invested and amazing life."

In fact, such a role sounds like a Jesus-honoring, Kingdom-producing life. I see that as CALLING. It is a bit contrary to the American ideal of being famous. We tell our children that they can do anything they want in life. In reality, we would serve them better by teaching them that they can have a life of significance by loving God and loving their neighbors in small ways. While connecting our children to their God-spoken identity, we need to teach them that significance is not found in accomplishments, acquisitions, or acclaim, but in worshipping God and using the influence we have been blessed to receive to bless others.

As Mother Theresa is quoted as saying, "We cannot do great things on this earth, only small things with great love."

A fourth misconception about calling is that there are sacred callings and then common work for those who do not receive such a sacred call. Somewhere in the practical theology of the middle ages, calling got hijacked for pastors, vicars, monks, and missionaries. These were holy professions that mandated calling, but the rest of humanity just found work. This was expressed in my years growing up as "high calling." I still have people say to me, "but you must be so fulfilled because you have a high calling." That is quite simply bad theology, and I hold historical church leaders responsible for creating this reflex in people. The doctrine of the priesthood of all believers certainly stands in the face of this misapplication of calling.

If you look at the biblical examples that I recounted on calling, very few were pastors or missionaries in the traditional sense of those roles. They were commodity traders, generals, shepherds, government officials, wine stewards, and farmers. The disciples' assignments as fishermen were just as much a high calling as that to become apostles and die for the faith. Paul's work as leather worker was as much a high calling as being a boundary-crossing missionary.

Everyone is called. Every vocation is a high calling, if it is your assigned vocation, and as long as it is work that honors God by following his commands to righteous living and a steward-ship that cares for people. I learned this by watching my own father. He was an executive with Bethlehem Steel Corporation when the steel industry still served as a major economic and developmental institute in America. He started out to train as a pastor. His father had been a pastor and so was my mother's father. However, they were stuck with a "higher calling" blind spot in which they could only envision calling through the lens of pastoral ministry.

It was difficult for my parents when they followed a different route. Their families could not understand them following a different life path. It was like they were abandoning the will of God for their lives. From my vantage point, my father would have been a terrible pastor. His gift base and anointing were not appropriate for that role. But he was a great worker in his office at Bethlehem Steel. I watched how every year he labored over hiring and layoff decisions because he knew they impacted families. I watched how he diligently served in his work. His day-to-day work was worship because he honored God in doing it with excellence, remaining a righteous presence in the work force. But he did not worship his work. He came home to be fully present with his family. He used his spare time to serve the church and the community. My Dad was called and he fulfilled his calling. The way he fulfilled his calling has made me a better minister of the Word, to fulfill my calling.

You have a calling. It is to be fully engaged in the Restoration Project where God has placed you. He has assignments for you in the day-to-day. Often those might seem mundane at the time, but they are uniquely part of the larger story that he is telling.

My only point in sharing these exchanges with others is to free you up from a type of spiritual roulette, trying to find God's will for your life by overthinking the process. We want to live an examined and purposeful life. We want to ask God for his assignments in life. We want to be fully alert to his opportunities to announce and demonstrate the Kingdom of God. The first step is to do what we know objectively of his declared will, which we can easily find in the Bible:

Start by loving God with all our being.

Add loving our neighbors as ourselves—beginning with our families and extending into our present communities of interaction.

Pray.

Be faithful in our present vocation.

Read Scripture and listen to the Holy Spirit for specific direction, while living in the accountability of a faith community.

And watch what God does!

I believe that getting strong in our primary call to God will then provide the space to experience his calling and guidance into the Somethings and Somewheres.

SO WHAT ARE MY NEXT STEPS?

You may already be actively living out your calling at this point in your life. However, you may want to more purposefully reflect on what your specific Something and Somewhere might be. As a pastor, I commonly hear, "So, how do you know what God's will is for my life?" I do believe that God is still calling and still guiding, and so he delights when we press him for more understanding or guidance. In the midst of being faithful to the principles noted above, if we want to gain a deeper understanding of our specific calling, we can advance to the next level of reflection.

If you have already received a radical childhood destiny calling, you do not need more counsel. Instead, you may need to dust it off or be renewed in the knowledge that God always finishes what he declares. If you have not received such a calling, don't just sit and wait for a bolt of lightning. While you are busy loving God and your neighbors in the place God has put you, a tool of discovery that can unlock your sense of calling is waiting for you.

If you have not yet received a clear sense of assignment, you may need a period of discernment to hone in on what calling means for you. In Appendix One of this book, you will find a model of reflection that I have developed. Set aside a morning or afternoon, where you can find some space of solace and reflection and walk through the suggested steps.

Scripture is pretty clear that God is not hiding and that he is a communicating God: "when you seek me you will find me" (Jeremiah 29:13). And even to his people who were living disconnected from his way, he stated,

> *"Whether you turn to the right or to the left, your ears will hear*
> *a voice behind you, saying, 'This is the way; walk in it'"*
> (Isaiah 30:21).

God wants you to find your renewed identity and Kingdom assignment more than you do. You are his son or daughter, and he cares deeply in your finding delight. And your delight is ultimately tied to your rescued identity and renewed assignment. Ravi Zacharias states it this way: "A calling is simply God's shaping of your burden and beckoning you to your service to him."[1] Bob Pierce, founder of World Vision, recognized calling as a heartbeat in tune to God's heartbeat. In her book *From Jerusalem to Irian Jaya*, Ruth A. Tucker quotes the motto Bob Pierce had inscribed in his Bible, the motto that summed up his life passion: "Let my heart be broken with the things that break the heart of God."[2]

There is an element of the surrender of control in this process. God will only work with what we willingly surrender to him. The prayer of David Livingston might be the best way to conclude this chapter:

> Lord, send me anywhere, only go with me;
> lay any burden on me, only sustain me;
> sever any ties but the ones that bind me to
> your service and your heart.[3]

May God give you courage to let go of your way and to press into his way. When you get to where you are able to fully surrender to his plan, you will then be ready to be commissioned with all of his resources to be successful in that calling.

PART IV

RESCUED FOR THE RESTORATION PROJECT: COMMISSIONED TO EXECUTE OUR CALLING

FROM THE BEGINNING of the biblical account we see the human race called into partnership with God. With the Fall, we walked away from God and from his purpose for us, severing that partnership with him. Through Christ, God offers us rescue to our true identity and brings us more fully back into the partnership with him. Having done so, he now sends us out to serve as his ambassadors of this Good News and to bring others into this restored relationship with God. This is our main role as partners with him—to join him in the Restoration Project.

When you get a new assignment in life there is the initial fear of the unknown. Each new chapter provides an opportunity for us to second-guess whether or not we have what it takes. When I worked as a landscaper as a teen all of it was new to me. I was intimidated initially: how deep to plant the sapling, how much water, what quantity of mulch. But as I learned the ins and outs of landscaping, I became more comfortable with the role. Then in graduate school I started my own landscaping business. I did the same with painting. As a freshman in college I answered an ad in the newspaper to paint someone's kitchen. I took the job so that I could buy Christmas presents before returning home to my family.

"Sure, I know how to paint," I reasoned. I had painted before, but this was my first venture into the world of working as a painter. I was nervous about getting it right and plied the hardware owner about right paint combinations for a kitchen. By the time I was in seminary, I had a partnership with a friend and we painted the exterior of five-story, multi-million-dollar houses. In each of those situations I had entered in over my head and had to learn.

The same has been true of my primary calling as a minister of the Word. Four years of undergrad and three years in seminary did not make me confident in pastoring my first church at age 25. Five years as a pastor did not make me confident in learning two languages and crossing cultural boundaries to become a missionary. Being a successful first term missionary did not make me feel ready to be the field director. Fifteen years of practical ministry were a good foundation to being a seminary professor, but I had to learn new ways of doing ministry. And then, how can one be adequately prepared to pastor a church in one of the most affluent communities in the world?

Even though there was a learning curve at each stage, I realized that my commission had come from God and he had given me everything I needed to be fruitful in that post. Here is some good news to go with the Good News: God empowers you with everything you need to be successful in his assignment for your life. You will need to develop the gifts he has given. You will need to work hard, be alert, and pray. But he has already set you up with the needed equipment.

After being chosen and called, recognizing the equipment with which God has commissioned us will give us courage and strength in carrying out our new assignments. Over the next chapters we will dive into the operational equipment that he gives us when he calls: his validation, his Kingdom authority, his power, and his proven method.

21

VALIDATED AS GOD'S SENT ONE

ONE OF THE MOST SIGNIFICANT THINGS I DO as a spiritual leader is validating others. I encounter those who have been rescued and who are becoming aware of their God-given calling(s) and assignments. With this awareness, the person then uses spiritual gifts, talents, time, resources, relationships—all get assumed into engaging their role in God's Restoration Project. Sometimes, though, they, and we, get stalled at the point of calling and fail to actually move out and fulfill that calling. What are we waiting for?

Validation.

We long for our leaders to commission us into our calling, to confirm to us that we have correctly heard God's call for us. I saw this especially played out when I was a seminary professor. My assignment was primarily to teach, to invite transformation in the lives of students by equipping them with new information and by modeling the ways of ministry. However, I began to notice that one of the most significant things I did was validating students into their calling—whether as pastors, missionaries, developmental workers, or even as well-trained lay leaders for the church, who found their vocation outside of the church. For whatever reason, students had not experienced validation from their parents or from other authorities in their lives. And even though most of those students had a sense of calling—that is why they were in seminary to receive training—they still lacked validation. Even the validated can sometimes be uncertain.

Although God's validation is more important than that of any human, sometimes we hear God's validation through the voice of others. The best place to arrive at in life is where we are secure in his validation and are no longer driven by the need for the validation and praise of others. Sometimes this sense of validation from God begins with a clear sense of Commission from our earthly models, mentors, and leaders. However, the best place to begin the validation process is with an understanding that God chooses to work through his people. He chooses to work through me and through you. He is not a hoarder of purpose but is always pushing ministry out away from himself.

Quite simply, God is a sending God. Sending is the overflow of his nature as a going and pursuing God. He crosses every type of boundary in order to express his love to us. God the Son, incarnate in Jesus, displayed most profoundly this boundary crossing character of the Triune God. He left heaven to come to earth. He emptied himself of divine privilege to take on limitations of humanity (Philippians 2:5-11). He left richness to become poor so that we might become rich (II Corinthians 8:9). Jesus declared over and over that he himself was sent—he was an ambassador from God the Father:

"Whoever receives me receives the one who sent me " (John 13:20).

"I came from the Father" (John 16:28).

"What I have heard from the Father I have made known to you" (John 15:15).

"Having accomplished the work you [the Father] gave me to do" (John 17:4).

Jesus was not just a sent one; he too was a sender. He began the sending process early in his ministry. He sent out the Twelve to do the very things he had been doing: announcing the kingdom, healing the sick, and casting out demons (Mark 6; Luke 9). He then extended the sending out to the Seventy-Two (Luke 10). Again, this sending was the natural overflow of the divine character of love, which pursues. God continues to pursue by sending out his people. English poet Francis Thomas captured this notion of the pursuing God in his classic poem "The Hound of Heaven." It is not surprising then that God sends us, his rescued people, out as ambassadors. Jesus makes this continuing nature of sending clear: "As the Father has sent me, even so I am sending you" (John 20:21).

It is important to note that Jesus did not limit the commissioning process to those who had the privilege of experiencing his earthly ministry; he extends the commission to all those who would believe in him (John 14:12). And his commission to his followers was clearly to a boundary-crossing activity expressed in the Great Commission: "as you are going, make disciples" (Matthew 28:20) and "be my witnesses to the ends of the earth" (Acts 1:8). He makes it clear that his departure from earth would only magnify the breadth of sending. The Holy Spirit would descend and continue to send the followers of Jesus across boundaries as ambassadors.

This sending is exactly what takes place in an ambassadorship. The Apostle Paul gives our divine assignment this name in his second letter to the Corinthians: "Therefore we are ambassadors for Christ, God making his appeal through us..." (II Corinthians 5:20). Ambassadors have no power of their own. They can only represent the sovereignties that have commissioned them to act on the sender's behalf. Having lived internationally for ten years I have seen this work of ambassadors operationalized in the natural world through government representatives. An ambassador is always aware of speaking in the name of the one who commissioned him or her. Likewise, an ambassador for Christ is always careful to speak on behalf of Christ.

You have the full force of God's stamp of approval on your life. He says to each Christ-bought son and daughter, I am validating you as a sent one. This God-given role of ambassador for God's Kingdom should, in itself, validate our call. But beyond his word of affirmation are all the aspects of the kingdom that undergird that assignment. In the Kingdom of God, Jesus is the King, and the force behind our mission is the force of his

Kingdom. He entrusts that Kingdom authority to us as we serve as stewards or ambassadors of the Kingdom. We will look more closely at these in the next chapter.

Would God set out on a plan that was lacking? This is his plan—to partner with us, to send us. But we still might second-guess our position or role. So it is good to return and rehearse what he has done to make us ready for his assignments. His validation is the backdrop to it all.

First, you were created exactly the way God wanted you to be. He has known you since the womb. You are fearfully and wonderfully made. He dances over you with exuberant delight.

Second, he has ordained your times and places so that you would find him. Nothing is lost in his plan. He has a way of assuming it all into your destiny.

Third, you were given you a new identity in Christ when he rescued you. You do not need to make a name for yourself. He has given you a new name and it is so precious to him that he has written it on his hands.

Fourth, he likes to remind you by his Holy Spirit how precious you are to him. He whispers *Abba Father* to your heart. He bears witness to us that we are forgiven. He reminds you that your adoption gives you full inheritance in his Kingdom family.

Fifth, he stands as guarantee of your ongoing development into becoming fully like Christ. He will bring it to completion. He will sanctify you wholly—body, soul, and spirit.

Sixth, he has prepared works in advance for you to do. He wants your engaged will but it is his might that will bring the results. He has already positioned people around you and will be ordaining your movements so that others can experience his love.

Seventh, God does not lie, so you can count on it.

All of those declarations come directly from Scripture, God's Word. You can see the passages attached to each phrase in Appendix Two. It is up to you whether you will agree with God's declaration over you. That validation is permanent and essential. This is important because other people might not always be present to validate our callings. Think back over the callings that I described from Scripture. Those callings were met with lots of opposition, not just in circumstances to overcome, but in the voices of people who were to benefit from the calling. Add to this that we have an active enemy of our soul, who accuses us non-stop. We need a strong dose of, and agreement with, God's validation over us.

Validated in that calling, we can then take hold of our kingdom authority.

22

SENT WITH KINGDOM AUTHORITY

AS AMBASSADORS we are operating as sent ones, validated and authorized by God himself. This means that we have the full force of his Kingdom authority behind us. When my wife and I lived internationally, it was quite easy to see which government held the greatest presence in ambassadorship in that land. Clues included size of embassy, presence of military, sound bites of the ambassador on television, and the weight of the ambassador's voice in international discussions. The Kingdom of God does not have a physical embassy, yet it carries the greatest weight of authority through its dispersed ambassadors.

The coming of Jesus meant a new unleashing of this Kingdom of God.

John the Baptist, in preparing those who would receive Jesus, declared the message, "The time has come; the Kingdom of God is near" (Mark 1:15). Jesus affirmed John the Baptist's message (Luke 16:16) and he proclaimed the good news of the Kingdom (Luke 8:1). The central message of Jesus was "the kingdom of God is at hand" (Matthew 4:17). Jesus was restoring the world back toward a God-given order. Jesus declared, "I must preach the good news of the kingdom of God, because that is **why I was sent**" (Luke 4:43). The Kingdom is referenced over ninety times in the gospels alone.

Jesus moved beyond proclaiming the kingdom of God, however, to demonstrating that it was already here. Luke 4:14-21 is viewed as Jesus's public declaration of his role in visibly advancing the Kingdom of God on earth. In this account, Jesus was in the synagogue in his hometown of Nazareth and was called upon to read the Scripture for the day, a passage from Isaiah 61. The Isaiah passage describes various manifestations of the presence of God's Kingdom, including anointing by the Holy Spirit, preaching good news, releasing the oppressed, healing, and experiencing God's favor. After reading the passage, Jesus declared, "Today, this scripture is fulfilled in your hearing" (4:21).

He then initiated a ministry that demonstrated the coming of this Kingdom, a ministry that emerged through a three-fold plan of action: preaching or announcing the Kingdom, healing, and casting out demons.

He said, "If I drive out demons by the finger of God, then the Kingdom of God has come" (Luke 10:20). The importance of these evidences of the Kingdom is seen in Jesus's response to the envoy of followers from John the Baptist, sent while John was in prison. John was seeking reassurance that he had not mistaken Jesus's identity and the coming of the Kingdom, so he sent a delegation to Jesus. Jesus told the messengers to go back to John with a description of what they had seen and heard—the preaching of the good news *and* its demonstration through healing (Matthew 11:1-5). Even the one whom Jesus called the greatest prophet of all, needed reassurance that his spiritual antennae were correct when things turned out differently than he had expected.

Now it would be easy for us to stop at this point and say, "Well, that was Jesus." Of course he announced and demonstrated the new Kingdom. We must remember, however, that Jesus passed on to his followers this calling to announce and demonstrate the Kingdom, and they were commissioned with the same action plan:

> *When Jesus had called the Twelve together, he gave them power and authority to drive out all demons and to cure diseases, and he sent them out to preach the kingdom of God and heal the sick* (Luke 9:1-2).

Later, when the seventy-two were sent out, they too were "to heal the sick" and announce that "the kingdom of God has come near" (10:9), and when they returned, they rejoiced because even the demons had been submitting to them (10:17). All three aspects of the commission were present—proclaim, heal, deliver.

During his earthly ministry, Jesus re-instituted the reign

of God on earth through his people. This meant taking up the authority which God had originally delegated to humanity and which humans had previously forfeited. When we forfeited God's authority, a new, usurped, authority structure was established. Jesus had to actively oppose this usurped authority structure. This was the turning point in the restoration process that is described in fullness in the Apocalypse of Revelations. Jesus then sent his followers out, not so much to establish the Kingdom, but to announce and demonstrate its reality. Only God can establish his kingdom—but he clearly chooses to do this through the lives of his people. Partnership!

As we move out to announce God's Kingdom and to let God establish his Kingdom through us, we are going to encounter conflict. Satan, the ruler of this age, does not want to turn over what he has stolen or overtaken, and he will not give it up easily. Thus, we enter into spiritual warfare. The biblical record shows this backdrop of warfare: darkness versus light. Jesus is said to have come "to destroy the works of the devil" (I John 3:8). He pushed back darkness by releasing kingdom-of-light works: disorientation was replaced with new identity; sickness was replaced with healing; bondage was replaced with freedom; and shalom or overall wellbeing became the new provision for the hard pressed. Jesus sealed the victory against these damaging effects by triumphing over Satan on the cross (Colossians 2:15) and through resurrection (Romans 1:4).

As commissioned ambassadors, we become the warriors in this ongoing battle to demonstrate Christ's victory. We are reminded in the Word to fight as a "good soldier of Christ Jesus" (II Timothy 2:3); to resist the devil (James 4); to put on our spiritual armor in order to stand against "the schemes of the devil" (Ephesians 6); and to advance with weapons that "are not of the flesh but have divine power to destroy strongholds" (II Corinthians 10). The Kingdom of God in us battles against the kingdom of darkness that rules in our world.

Given the warfare nature of our task and the ferociousness of our enemy, it is empowering to know that we are not out there on our own. Our calling and our ability to fulfill that calling do not result from our own effort; they come from the flow of Christ's life through us. When we operate fully in our mission—that to which he (co)missioned us—we have the full force of the Kingdom of God behind our movements. This is similar to the situation of an ambassador in a foreign country; such an ambassador does not have the resources or the power within self to impact change in that country, but he or she does have a great opportunity to enact change by bringing to bear the resources and power of the American government he or she represents. When we are on mission with God, we bring the full reign of God into the situations and circumstances of that calling. We are Kingdom ambassadors.

In this struggle, we know that the victory is guaranteed in the war. However, we still are living out daily skirmishes or battles. Because we are in the in between times – the first coming and the second coming of Jesus – we sometimes receive blows or even feel at times like darkness is winning. The kingdom of God is here but not in the full sense of heaven's rule. This is why we pray for God's kingdom to come and his will to be done on earth as it is in heaven. This is why we continue to fight. The kingdom is here but not yet – we get demonstration of it but not completely.

As we observe the Kingdom of God released in and through

our lives, our sense of calling becomes validated. As Kingdom ambassadors we do not experience only success. In fact, the promise of Scripture is that we would experience opposition and even persecution in this role. So we do not just live by what is immediately seen. Instead, when we move in Kingdom understanding, we are able to look back over our lives to see the evidence of Kingdom release. This validation inspires us to keep moving boldly in our Kingdom calling even as new opposition manifests.

It is key to note that the validation from God is not merely in verbal confirmation of our standing. Validation is substantive. God actually gives us his authority to act. He wants us to take hold of it, appropriate it, and to use it.

To understand the nature of the spiritual authority with which we operate, we need to go back to the beginning of God's Big Story. When God created Adam and Eve (humanity), he placed them in a position of authority over the rest of creation. This authority is described in the notions of **ruling** and **subduing**:

> Then God said, "Let us make man in our image, in our likeness, and let them **rule** over..."
> So God created man in his own image...male and female he created them.
> God blessed them and said to them, "Be fruitful and increase in number; fill the earth and **subdue** it. **Rule** over..."
> (Selections from Genesis 1:26-28).

This ruling and subduing were rooted in a deep sense of stewardship rather than in exploitation or abuse. This was to be our heritage. Being created in the image of God means that we were designed to rule in the same manner as he does, in a way that is always beneficial for the other—*not* through manipulation or abusive control.

When Adam and Eve chose to obey Satan instead of God, they, to some degree, gave Satan legal right to rule on the earth. It is not my purpose to go into detail regarding the narrative of the Fall (Genesis 3). I will simply note that the order God created out of chaos was turned back to chaos through an usurped authority structure. The serpent in the narrative (Satan and the kingdom of darkness) tempted Adam and Eve (humanity) to operate in a system other than the original design. As a result, humans gave up the authorized role that God had given them to rule and reign.

Jesus entered the world to rectify this forfeited calling. He operated with a new sense of authority. Scripture repeatedly tells us how people observed him operating out of this new Kingdom reality with authority: he taught with authority, cast out demons with authority, healed with authority, and even commanded nature with authority. This authority progressed throughout Christ's earthly life and beyond, when, after his ascension, he takes his place of authority on the throne. Peter too speaks of this authority of Christ. Writing to believers who were being challenged on every side and who were, by all outward appearances, losing the battle, he reminds them that Jesus "has gone into heaven and is at God's right hand—with angels, authorities and powers in submission to him" (I Peter 3:22). Paul explains that Jesus had realigned the structure of rule so that all powers and authorities were under his feet:

> *"...his incomparably great power for us who believe. That power*
> *is the same as the mighty strength he exerted when he raised*
> *Christ from the dead and seated him at his right hand in*
> *the heavenly realms, far above all rule and authority, power*
> *and dominion, and every name that is invoked, not only in*
> *the present age but also in the one to come. And God placed*
> *all things under his feet and appointed him to be head over*
> *everything for the church, which is his body, the fullness of*
> *him who fills everything in every way"* (Ephesians 1:19-23).

This realignment is encouraging in itself. But Paul goes on to point out that this positioning of Christ on the throne directly correlates to the spiritual position that we have as Christ ambassadors. After celebrating our rescue from darkness (Ephesians 2:1-5), Paul goes on to state, "And God raised us up with Christ and seated us with him in the heavenly realms in Christ Jesus." (2:6)

This is the pivotal Bible verse on spiritual authority as it relates to the Christ follower. The tense used by Paul in this declaration is significant. We expect Paul to say that one day ***we will be*** seated with him. That is the "not yet" expectation of the Kingdom: we long for his Kingdom to come! However, Paul uses the present perfect tense: he *has raised* us up and *has seated* us with Christ; these are completed actions with ongoing effects. **We are seated with him.** Already done!

Since those early believers who received the original letter from Paul were not already physically present at the throne of Jesus—neither are we—what was Paul saying? He was referring to our **spiritual** position. This means that in this intermediate time—the kingdom of "now but not yet"—authorities, powers, and dominions are already underneath our feet. We are called to take up the authority reclaimed for us and to bring to completion what Jesus has already established.

This helps us understand the intent of the writer of Hebrews when he describes the completed enthronement: "he sat down at the right hand" (past tense, already completed), and the incomplete subjugation: "he waits for his enemies to be made his footstool" (present tense, continuing action) (Hebrews 10:12-13). From the perspective of spiritual authority, in Christ we are already endued with Kingdom authority. From a historical perspective, Christ followers are invited into the process of reigning with Christ by taking hold of this authority and re-establishing our rightful rule, God's reign, on earth. What the king declares, we the ambassadors carry out in his name for the places and people that still remain outside of his rule.

When Jesus commissions us, we have the spiritual authority to demonstrate that Kingdom. What is this authority?

> Spiritual authority is the God-given right of rulership, rooted in relationship with Him through Christ, whereby we superimpose the rules, order, and impact of His world (the kingdom of God) over our world.[1]

As participants in this war between God's kingdom of light and Satan's kingdom of darkness, we battle all types of competing authorities, powers, and dominions. Spiritual authority in Christ trumps all of these. As these powers attempt to block the advance of God's kingdom, we are to exert our authority as ambassadors to accomplish the King's rule. We take authority over all aspects of the flesh, the world, and the kingdom of darkness that oppose the knowledge of God and the release of his Kingdom in our world. So, to be commissioned means to be authorized by the most powerful kingdom and to be empowered with the authority of the King.

23

ENERGIZED ON MISSION WITH HOLY SPIRIT POWER

COUPLED WITH THIS SPIRITUAL AUTHORITY is empowerment by the Holy Spirit. We see this modeled first of all in the ministry of Jesus. His public ministry did not begin until the descent of the Holy Spirit upon him at his baptism (Luke 3:21-22). Immediately after describing this event Luke writes, "Jesus himself was about thirty years old when he began his ministry" (2:23). Jesus made it clear as to how he operated with power: "by the Spirit of God" (Matthew 12:28) and "by the finger of God" (Luke 11:20). Luke describes Jesus's power, not as power that Jesus exerted of his own will, but as power that was released at chosen times: "One day the power of the Lord was present for him to heal the sick" (Luke 5:17). The implication of this passage is that the previous day, or some other day, the power was not present. Peter, in a talk to a group gathered in the home of Cornelius, also describes Jesus being empowered by the Holy Spirit:

> *"You know what has happened throughout Judea, beginning in Galilee after the baptism that John preached – how God anointed Jesus of Nazareth with the Holy Spirit and power, and how he went around doing good and healing all who were under the power of the devil, because God was with him"* (Acts 10:37-38).

Jesus operated in power as the outflow of his anointing by the Holy Spirit. Jesus promised his followers a similar dynamic through the outpouring of the Holy Spirit. In the Upper Room discourses (John 14-16), Jesus told his followers that it was good for him to leave them, as he would be sending a Helper, the Holy Spirit, who would do all things through them. Before his ascension, he told them that this would include POWER for the mission before them. "You will receive power when the Holy Spirit comes upon you and you will be my witnesses in Jerusalem, Judea and Samaria, and to the ends of the earth" (Acts 1:8). Once again we hear ambassador language. We are sent out to represent Christ, to be witnesses to him, to be his ambassadors; through the Holy Spirit, though, we become ambassadors endued with power.

The power of God through the Holy Spirit was not new

with Jesus. The prophet Zechariah had made it clear that true success could only be found in the Spirit of God. "Not by might, nor by power, but by my Spirit, says the Lord of hosts" (Zechariah 4:6). But before the coming of Christ, an expansion of the release of this power was expected. The prophet Joel looked forward to the day when the Lord would "pour out his Spirit on all flesh" (Joel 2:28). Whereas God had worked by his Spirit primarily through God's leaders during the old covenants, the day was expected when empowerment would come for all. That day was Pentecost (Acts 2). The expectation of the prophet Joel and the promise of power from Jesus were united at the release of the Holy Spirit upon the newly formed church.

This pouring out of the Spirit upon them changed the dynamism of the early believers. Their hope had been restored by the appearances of the resurrected Christ. Then their lives were transformed by the baptism and filling of the Holy Spirit. This filling has been passed down to all ambassadors in Christ. To be in Christ is to have the indwelling Holy Spirit (Romans 8:9-11) and to have the power that comes through the Spirit (Ephesians 1:19-20; 3:20-21).

How do we tap into this power? Believers are encouraged to cooperate with the Spirit. Paul commands followers to *keep on* being filled with the Holy Spirit (Ephesians 5:18). Paul's use of verb tense shows that there is a constant abiding in and yielding to the filling process. His choice of Greek words also connects this filling to an image of power. He uses a nautical term to express the filling. The image is that of a fully open sail being filled with wind to push the vessel forward through the water. Knowing that the Hebrew word for the Spirit is *ruah*, meaning both "wind" and "breath," adds to the image. The invitation in our (co)mission is to open our sails to the wind of the Holy Spirit and to be empowered by the Spirit, pushed forward toward the fulfillment of our calling.

A quick look at the progression of being Chosen, Called, and Commissioned reveals that it is a Holy-Spirit-saturated process. The Spirit makes us aware of our chosen-ness. The Spirit bears witness to Jesus (John 15:26). The Spirit then convicts of sin (John 16:8) and alerts us to the fact that we are at enmity with God because of our sin, a step that is necessary if we are to take advantage of the Rescue God offers. Paul states that it is also by the Spirit that we move from being aliens and strangers back into a right relationship with God. Through Jesus Christ we "have access in one Spirit to the Father" (Ephesians 2:18). The Spirit is also said to circumcise the heart (Romans 2:29), give new birth (John 3:5), give life (John 6:63), and save and renew us (Titus 3:5). In addition to this, he seals his work in us (II Corinthians 1:22, 5:5) and affirms for our doubting hearts that we are truly adopted as God's children (Romans 8:16).

"God has sent the Spirit of his Son into our hearts, crying 'Abba! Father!'" (Galatians 4:6).

It is the Spirit who reveals God's calling and commissions us for action. In Acts 13, we see this clearly in the sending of Barnabas and Saul (Paul). The church was in a time of fasting, prayer, and worship, when the Spirit said to them, "Set apart for me Barnabas and Saul for the work to which I have called them" (Acts 13:2). The church was the sending agent, working alongside the Holy Spirit. The church confirmed the word from the Holy Spirit and laid hands on Paul and Barnabas to send them off (13:3). The import of the sending by the church is confirmed by the sense of accountability that these first two missionaries showed in returning to the church to report their actions (Acts 14:27). The sending, however, was first initiated by the Holy Spirit. In fact, Acts 13:4 states boldly that they were "being sent out by the Holy Spirit." Paul later shows that it was through the Holy Spirit that he identified closed and open doors in the mission as the work of God (Acts 16:6, 10).

The Holy Spirit's part in validating our call does not end at the giving of the call; his presence is a continual affirmation of the commission. In addition to empowering us, the Holy Spirit also equips us to fulfill the call and brings about the results. The Spirit releases fruit (Galatians 5), gives gifts for ministry (I Corinthians 12, Romans 12), prays through us (Romans 8:26-27, Ephesians 6:18, Jude 20), anoints (Acts 10:38, II Corinthians 1:21-22, I John 2:20), takes up residence (I Corinthians 3:16, 6:19), and sanctifies over and over (Galatians 5:16; I Peter 1:2). Thus, in our partnership with God we are exhorted to cooperate with the Spirit's work, to eliminate anything in our lives that would hinder the Spirit's work (Ephesians 4:30, I Thessalonians 5:19). This connection with the Holy Spirit elicits boldness (Acts 4:31) and joy (Acts 13:52), each validating God's call on our lives.

Once we realize the impact of having our lives full of God's power we simply then maintain connection to the Spirit (Ephesians 5:18) and remain in step with where the Spirit is moving (Galatians 5:25). He will guide us into our Restoration Project assignments.

In the same way that the descent of the Holy Spirit inaugurated Jesus into his ministry, the "descent" of the Holy Spirit upon us gives us everything we need for our mission. When we operate in our God-given role as ambassadors and we exercise the authority that accompanies that role, we operate in the power of the Holy Spirit, and a demonstration of the transforming life of the Kingdom of God is released through us for the benefit of others. Chosen, called, commissioned—all of the work of God and the overflow of God is channeled through us to establish the Restoration Project.

24

EQUIPPED WITH A JESUS-PROVEN METHODOLOGY

AS AMBASSADORS WE REPRESENT GOD'S KINGDOM. Thus, as God's ambassadors we must operate in God's way; our methods of going forth in this mission must reflect his methods. In addition, the methods used to convey the message cannot be contrary to the message. The message is that God loves us and will cross any boundaries necessary to express that love to us through rescuing us, and that he will then use us to rescue others. This is the same message embodied in Jesus's life in the world. Scripture shows us that Christ used three types of encounters to convey his message: love, truth, and power. Another way of describing these encounters is as Kingdom interventions expressed through incarnation, proclamation, and demonstration.

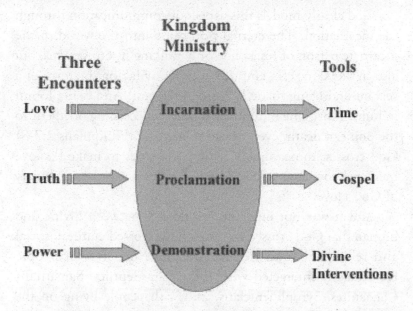

These three encounters become the model Christ followers are to use on their mission to communicate God's Good News.

INCARNATION

Incarnation is a commitment to model the message before and as we speak. Incarnation is inviting people to experience God's love through our actions before putting words to the message. People need to know that we care about them before they will hear about our caring message. Thus, there is an important question to ask before sharing Good News with someone: "Is this relationship a strong enough bridge to bear the weight of the heavy truth I am about to share?" The Good News can be very heavy for someone separated from God's love.

God clearly models this aspect of communication through the incarnation. The eternal Son came into the world in the incarnate person of Jesus, not only walking in our sandals, but also in our skin. He "emptied himself by taking the form of a servant and being made in human likeness. And being found in human form, he humbled himself by becoming obedient to the point of death, even death on a cross" (Philippians 2:7-8). God crosses immeasurably wide boundaries to make his love message known to us. He embodied it. Jesus was the vocabulary of God's love.

And it was not only the boundaries between divine and human that God crossed in Jesus. Jesus crossed cultural, social, and religious boundaries to enter into the lives of people. He regularly interacted with the pagan Gentiles: Samaritans, Canaanites, Syrophoenicians, and with people living on the "other side." When at his hometown synagogue of Nazareth he announced his coming as fulfillment of the Messianic expectation of Isaiah 61 people were awed. However, they became angry and turned violent when he illustrated that Messianic hope by using examples of Gentiles experiencing God's power through ancient prophets (Luke 4).

Jesus also crossed social boundaries through his interactions with women and the marginalized, who, being religiously unclean, were separated socially from others. He reached out across many boundaries: touching lepers, touching the dead, and spending time with sinners and tax collectors. All that time, he was fully present in the lives of the people he came to save. His message was not launched from a distance, but was lived out in the everyday of human interaction.

The disciples learned this unique approach and went out with the same determination to be engaged with people in their local and daily realities. Jesus had told them to go out to a town, find a person of peace, and stay with them. They followed the Jesus way, traveling across many boundaries, to be incarnational witnesses to Jesus.

Paul's ministry is the most described ministry in the New Testament apart from that of Jesus, and incarnation was clearly the foundation of his approach. He wrote to the church in Thessalonica, "We were ready to share with you not only the gospel of God but also our own selves" (I Thessalonians 2:8). So engrafted was Paul in the settings where he traveled that he could later say to the same church, "Imitate me as I imitate Christ" (II Thessalonians 3:7, 9). Paul declared, "I have become all things to all people, that by all means I might save some" (I Corinthians 9:22). The implication here is that purposeful cultural and social saturation with contextualization can take away unnecessary stumbling blocks to the Good News.

In the same way that Jesus was the vocabulary of God, we become the ongoing expression of God's love by the way we live our own lives. I have lived on three continents for extended periods of time and have ministered on another three. In each place, the efforts that I made to minister via incarnation made all the difference in how people were able to receive the message that I proclaimed. In order to communicate God's love in these places I needed to enter their world to such a degree that I earned the right to have a hearing. In France and Mali, it meant not only learning to speak the languages of the people, but it also meant learning their worldview and the social rules of how and when to communicate. The right words in the wrong way can be as disastrous as using the wrong words. Even when traveling internationally for short periods of time I have tried to learn the social rules and cultural-historical connection points of the gospel.

As an adult I have also lived in three distinctive areas of America. In each of those places, I have tried to take the same approach as I did internationally: becoming like the people to whom I hoped to bring Good News. This has required incarnational living—being with people in order to get the right to dialogue with them about faith, and building a strong, culturally and socially appropriate bridge to bear the weight of heavy truth.

We must remember that on mission we are inviting people into a relationship with God. We are not trying to convince them of the religious truths that we believe or to get them to adopt our religious system. Good News is about reconciliation— restored relationship—with God, with others, and with self. In the same way that the method of mission cannot be contrary to the message, the message of renewed relationship is best transmitted within a shared relationship. This type of relationship is implied in the words of Peter: "always being prepared to make a defense to anyone who asks you for a reason for the hope that is in you" (I Peter 3:15). A person needs to be in contact with you enough to see that hope. That is incarnational mission and the task to which the church is commissioned.

Sometimes as people on mission, in our passion to help people reconnect to God, we may give the impression that they are an evangelism project. That will not work. People sense when we are interested in them because we have an ulterior motive. Besides, such an approach would be contrary to the incarnational model of Jesus. He loved people just to love them, not on the basis of how they responded to him. He healed ten lepers; only one came back to thank him. He prayed for his killers on the cross—"forgive them, for they know not what they do." People gained a sense of dignity around Jesus because he touched them in their pain and he was fully present to them in his interaction. People need to be loved simply because they are people. This kind of love is not saturated with angst over whether the other person accepts Good News or not; still, it does rejoice with great delight when Good News lands.

This focus on incarnational ministry can be a relief to many of us as we consider our place in the Restoration Project. The majority of us are not called to go live in a foreign culture. God has placed us where we live now to incarnate in our own culture. Our boundary crossing is from the spaces of belief to unbelief. Mission happens at the meeting of the people of God and the not-yet-people of God. In our crossing boundaries in these places we often get to use what is familiar to us as a bridge for the Good News. We naturally gather with people who have same interests and/or social situations for life. God wants us to be fully alert in those everyday relationships to be his ambassadors of love. It simply means being present and being sources of practical love for those around us. Even ministering in familiar spaces requires that we spend time in creative reflection on boundary crossing.

Understanding the importance of incarnational aspects of ministry also has a way of redeeming our suffering and challenging circumstances. I have observed that the gospel shines as much and even more through the person who suffers with hope in such a way that he reflects a confidence in God in spite of pain. I have observed that the gospel shines brilliantly through people who endure in the face of challenging circumstances. I have observed the gospel shine brilliantly in places where forgiveness was given to "undeserving" enemies or critics. Sometimes that reflection of God's love is even greater than when we get to pray a miracle into someone's life.

One of my favorite statements on witness is from I Peter 3:15, *"always being prepared to make a defense to anyone who asks you for* a reason *for the hope that is in you."* I think this is a good strategy. Live with so much hope that people are curious about why we are so hopeful. Now this phrase is most profound when the context of hopefulness is suffering, challenging circumstances, and direct opposition. So if my life is going well—I have a nice home, my family is doing well, I drive a nice car, I get to take great vacations, and so forth—people are not going to look at me with curiosity because I have hope. But if my life experiences are challenging and I have hope, then they are going to be more curious about the source of that hope. Suffering and challenging circumstances are to be embraced as places where the gospel might shine most brilliantly from my life.

PROCLAMATION

Proclamation is the message itself. Jesus announced that the Kingdom of God was at hand. He proclaimed a new way, a way saturated in God's love. He proclaimed a fresh way of looking at God's kingdom presence, and accompanied the proclamation with a call to operate in the new ethic of that kingdom. Jesus passed that same message on to his followers. Working to incarnate a message in a culturally and socially appropriate manner is useless if the message is not worth telling. This is the easiest part of our co(mission)—we have a message worth telling; we bring Good News.

While we bring Good News, I remind us again that **how** we communicate this message can cause it to be received as either good news or bad news. The truth of the matter is that our message of Good News does have an element of bad news within it. Humanity needs rescue, which essentially means we are lost. But telling someone that they are lost is not always the best starting point for communicating the Good News—it might create more frustration than thankfulness.

The Apostle Paul modeled this contextual proclamation approach well with the Athenians at the Areopagus (Acts 17). The Areopagus was a place where philosophers gathered daily to converse. Paul did not walk into their gathering and decry their philosophies as useless. This would have driven them away or would have, at least, discouraged further communication. Instead, he began by first understanding at what point they were. He first thought about the Athenians: what were their starting points? He then began his proclamation of the Good News by using those starting points: commending them as being very religious (17:22), referring to what they already believed—"even some of your own poets have said" (17:28), and addressing what they already worshipped as the "unknown god" (17:23). Wisely, Paul began with concepts of God as creator of all and sovereign over all before moving to newer and more complicated notions of resurrection and the Lordship of Jesus. In doing so, Paul was allowing the Good News to emanate out of the Athenians' own assumptions about life.

The study of the history of the missionary movement, along with more recent insights from the social sciences, has enhanced this understanding of communications. It has always been a temptation for missionaries to bring their culture with their message. This temptation likely grows out of the fact that we cannot experience faith apart from our cultures and worldviews. Jesus, the Good News, the Kingdom of God, and salvation—all of these notions of our faith come to us from a particular historical and cultural setting. In fact, the message is complete nonsense without the culture in which it was given to us. Likewise, we cannot receive that message apart from the filters of our own worldview and culture. I cannot "de-shell" the message like a peanut to reveal a core understanding that stands outside of culture. Shell is culture and peanut is essence—there is no peanut without shell.

There is no way of passing the message on in a type of cultureless expression. However, the Christian faith has a remarkable ability to be translated into many cultures without losing its feeling of ancient orthodoxy. Though Jesus was a first-century Palestinian Jew, one does not have to take on the language and customs of first-century Judaism to be a Christ follower. Somehow Jesus does not get lost when he dresses in different clothes and eats different foods—he still feels quite authentic in every culture in which he is made manifest by his people. All this exhorts us to think about our own worldview and the cultural assumptions that we bring to the moment of witness.

Even beyond the cultural aspect of the message, we need to be aware that the message gets encoded from the starting point of our underlying motivations and attitudes, which then bleed into the proclamation. If I begin with the lost-ness of man, I might have the tendency to talk down to people. However, if my motivation is what Paul declares as love, then my encoding of the message might come from a different angle. In the passage where Paul reminds us of our commissioning as ambassadors—God making his appeal through us, he also states what our motivation should be: "the love of Christ compelling us" (II Corinthians 5:14). Earlier in this same letter, Paul called followers of Christ to be the "aroma of Christ" (II Corinthians 2:15). We should consider the implications of this metaphor: aroma enhances, is subtle, and does not assault the senses.

Scripture declares that the message we are to proclaim, the Good News of Jesus, is "the power of God for salvation to everyone who believes, to the Jew first and also to the Greek" (Romans 1:16). This power gets released when spiritual eyes of the heart have been enlightened to understand the message. We know from Scripture, though, that the enemy of our souls is trying to block that light:

> *"And even if our gospel is veiled, it is veiled to those who are perishing. In their case the god of this world has blinded the minds of the unbelievers, to keep them from seeing the light of the gospel of the glory of Christ, who is the image of God"* (II Corinthians 4:3-4).

Thus, spiritual warfare is added to the complex cultural and attitudinal barriers already affecting our proclamation of the message. Before we speak and even while we are speaking, we are praying. It is prayer for guidance to get the words and message correct. And it is warfare prayer to pull blinders off of the receivers and to be alert to the individuals over whom the Holy Spirit is already hovering.

Added to the cultural, attitudinal, and spiritual dynamic is the natural challenge of the message itself. How do we explain to would-be followers Jesus's sobering words: that they must take up the cross and follow him? It is not an easy message to take in. Paul is describing this challenge when he writes, "Christ crucified [is] a stumbling block to Jews and folly to Gentiles" (I Corinthians 1:23). In short, because Jesus Christ and his crucifixion is enough of a stumbling block, we should not add further obstacles by our own conduct in proclaiming the message or because of the way we package the message.

Paul, who was knowledgeable about the gospel, understood the complexity of and challenge in proclaiming the message. He alluded to this in his prayer request to the church in Colossae: "At the same time, pray also for us, that God may open a door for the word, to declare the mystery of Christ…that I may make it clear, which is how I ought to speak" (Colossians 4:3-4). We discussed earlier how, while in Athens, Paul met this challenge of proclaiming the message across boundaries. Paul was masterful in the way he interacted with philosophers at the Areopagus. However, we rarely hear about Paul's failures in communication.

His most glaring failure was in Lystra (Acts 14). He began with a powerful demonstration of healing, a method of kingdom ministry that in other settings had opened the door to the proclamation of the gospel. But in this instance, communication broke down, and the people resorted to conferring divine status to the two missionaries; they began worshipping Paul and Barnabas because of the miracle they'd performed, just as they'd been worshipping Zeus and Hermes. There is an interesting comment in the narrative that might help us understand the cause of the communication failure: it states that the people began speaking in Lycaonian. Though Paul spoke the imperial language, which his hearers understood, he did not know their heart language. In Paul's and Barnabas's frustration, they attempted to stop the worship by tearing their robes. Now this symbolic act would have been understood in Jerusalem, or among the well-trained Jews in diaspora. However, it was like a foreign language to the citizens of Lystra. As masterful as Paul was in Acts 17, we see that he learned that mastery through the failure described in Acts 14.

The accounts of Paul's failure can be an encouragement to us. Fulfilling our calling is not about getting it right. It is about being available to God. He has the ability to take our best and worst efforts and turn them into fruitfulness for his kingdom. This is not an excuse to refrain from thinking about how we communicate Good News. There are many good books that can give us insights into this process of verbal witness so that we can better communicate the Good News; we want to be trained well. However, the knowledge that God holds us accountable for our actions, and not for the reactions of others should take the pressure off of us. We are not responsible for the impact of the message. This is the work of the Holy Spirit. He merely wants us to join our witness to what he is already declaring.

I find the best method is to simply seed the Word of God in small doses. Rather than trying to unpack the whole gospel message, I like to throw out teasers in the midst of real, everyday conversation. "That reminds me of a parable that Jesus told." "There is a great proverb in the Bible that says the same thing." "That really is a challenging situation that has been around for a long time. Even Jesus dealt with it. His way of dealing was…" These snippets of the Word whet the appetite or speak to the spiritual thirst. They will cause people to want more. And using them gives space for the Holy Spirit to work because he says that his Word "will not return to me empty, but will accomplish what I desire and achieve the purpose for which I sent it" (Isaiah 55:11).

In these few short paragraphs we have highlighted the complexity of proclaiming the Good News. We never "just" communicate. Communication comes via multiple filters. Knowing the importance of the message, we would be wise to think about how we can best deliver it.

The realization of the need to communicate through a lens of cultural and social understanding has changed the way people talk about the church in America and Europe. We live in a post-Christian and postmodern world. The church in these geographic areas used to be able to communicate the Good News of Jesus with a sense that they shared a common worldview with their listeners. However, this is no longer the case. This divide between the Christian worldview and the secular worldview has grown with each generation. We are like Paul in Lystra or Athens. We need to think about the cultural filters through which we speak and through which the message will be received. In America, we are in a post-Christian and post-Christendom world. Our message needs to reflect that reality.

Added to this challenge of cross-cultural communication is the rapidly changing generational culture. Cultural observers suggest that today a new generation is born about every five years. Change and technology are creating escalating generational divides. These divides serve as cultural divides, or at least social divides, that impact communication. The message needs to be contextualized for each generation.

The present generations no longer have the same connection to the truth categories that have guided previous generations. They are more interested in experiential truth than propositional truth. One of the church's reflexes to this challenge of communicating clearly has been to suggest that we no longer need to proclaim the message. Instead, they say, we need only live the message. The quote commonly used to support this approach is from Francis of Assisi:

> Preach all the time and on every occasion and if necessary use words.

On the one hand, I love this quote because it shows the importance of incarnation alongside proclamation. However, I dislike the quote on the turn of one word: *if.* I would rephrase it this way:

> Preach all the time and on every occasion and WHEN necessary use words.

Good News has to be heralded, not only pantomimed. If I live the most Christ-like life ever observed on this earth, and yet do not add my words, I remain a testimony only to myself. It is through the verbal communication of the message that people are given the opportunity to learn about the source of the message, the source that would allow them also to live out their Rescued identity and Restored assignment in the Kingdom of God.

DEMONSTRATION

The third aspect of communication is demonstration. Demonstration is the display of power that serves as an exclamation point to the Good News. For Jesus, the kingdom announcement included the demonstration of healing the sick and casting out demons. As mentioned earlier, while in prison John the Baptist had some doubts about Jesus. John's experiences were causing him to second-guess his initial assessment of Jesus. So John sent a delegation to ask Jesus if he was indeed the Messiah, the Christ. Jesus answered by telling the delegation to report what they had heard and seen: "the blind receive their sight and the lame walk, lepers are cleansed and the deaf hear, and the dead are raised up, and the poor have good news preached to them" (Matthew 11:5). The affirmation of Christ and his teachings about the kingdom was in the demonstration.

The disciples followed the same pattern of ministry that Jesus did. We highlighted above how this went beyond the immediate twelve, and even beyond the initial seventy-two. The early church was submerged in divine intervention described as signs and wonders (Acts 2:43). In fact, one of the main points of Acts of the Apostles is that the work of Jesus is carried on through the followers of Jesus. We see this continuation of the works of Jesus in the experiences of Philip while he was on mission in Samaria to "proclaim to them Christ" (Acts 8:4). We are told that his message was heard not only because of the quality of the message, but also because of the demonstration of the Kingdom of God through "the signs that he did" (8:5). Miracles of both restoration and judgment affirmed that the Word of God was spreading.

The apostle Paul's missionary journeys were also laced

with power (Acts 13-28). Paul, when writing to the church in Corinth, noted that his speech and his message "were not in plausible words of wisdom, but in demonstration of the Spirit and of power...so that your faith might not rest on the wisdom of men but in the power of God" (I Corinthians 2:4-5). We know that he is not saying here that his message was unintelligible. Paul was an educated, wise man, and his writing reflect this reality. His point was that the acceptance of the message did not hinge solely on its delivery, but also relied on the accompanying release of power for healing, deliverance, and divine intervention. The release of Holy Spirit power saturates the whole process.

We are to continue to pray today for God's powerful intervention in the lives of people with whom we are sharing the Good News. Our message is only partially complete when we model it through intentional incarnational presence and when we formulate and proclaim it in a manner that is contextually sensitive to the audience. The message is most fully communicated in displays of power. We create spaces for God's powerful intervention through proactively praying for people and with people that they might experience that intervention.

At the beginning of the 1900s, a theology was constructed that took the demonstration of God's power out of the equation. Through an obscure interpretation of passages such as I Corinthians 12:8-10, a dispensational theology developed that stated that miracles ended in the time of the early church. The referenced verse from I Corinthians declares:

> *"Love never ends. As for prophecies, they will pass away; as for tongues, they will cease; as for knowledge, it will pass away.*

For we know in part and we prophesy in part, but when the perfect comes, the partial will pass away."

To interpret this passage as the passing away of miracles once the Word of God was canonized is a glaring hermeneutical weakness. It ignores the context of the passage, which goes on to say, "for now we see in a mirror dimly, but then face to face" (12:12). Clearly, in Pauline usage this is a description of glorification, when we are face to face with Jesus. Sadly, this faulty interpretation has led many Christ-followers to live with a limited understanding of and application of the power that God wants to release in and through us. Signs and wonders are still a part of his kingdom release through us. We rely on the signs, needing their direction until we reach our destination.

This weak hermeneutic also ignores the teaching of Jesus. Earlier we noted John 14 and the sending out of the followers of Christ:

"I tell you the truth, anyone who has faith in me will do what I have been doing. He will do even greater things than these, because I am going to the Father" (John 14:12).

Several elements of John 14:12 are interesting for the discussion on a demonstration of the Good News. Jesus offers the authority of the Kingdom of God to those well beyond the original twelve and the seventy-two, well beyond the New Testament church even. He offers it to **anyone** who is in a relationship with him. A dispensational approach to authority and power will not work at this point. We cannot reject the miracles of Jesus and the Bible merely as conventions of an ancient world that attributed spiritual reasons for natural phenomena. Nor can we believe that the miracles and manifestation of the Holy Spirit are no longer needed now that we have God's Word.

We can see how this would play out in the interpretation of John 14:12. If your theology does not allow for the miraculous, then you would need to weave an interpretative dance around the idea of "greater things." One proposed explanation of this passage attempts to re-interpret the delegated authority as unrelated to miracles, claiming that the "greater things" refers to acts of love (which applies I Corinthians 12 to this declaration of Jesus). Even if this is the case, there are still the words of Jesus in the previous verse, "Anyone who has faith in me will do what I have been doing." Two of the things that he clearly did, and repeatedly did, were to heal the sick and cast out demons.

We cannot get around the promise that we can act in authority, and in authority even do miracles. We must always read Scripture in its immediate context. When we do so here, we see that in verse 11, Jesus referenced the "**works themselves**" (John 14:11). The full verse makes the point even clearer: "Believe me that I am in the Father and the Father is in me [incarnation], or else believe on account of the works themselves [demonstration]." Jesus did not do miracles as a sideshow; they were a confirmation of the message he proclaimed. Demonstration was as essential as incarnation in making God's kingdom message discernable to the receiver. We see that the early followers of Christ moved in that same pattern. Historically, this has continued through the church, though it ebbs and flows for various reasons. Interestingly enough, it seems to flow most profoundly when the church is on mission, crossing boundaries into the lives of the people who have not yet experienced Good News.

Demonstration is still a valuable part of the communication process. All three aspects of communicating the Good News are needed if we are to fulfill our part in God's Restoration Project: Incarnation, Proclamation, and Demonstration.

So, how does Demonstration happen? By creating space to invite God to work in someone's life. Let's begin with the example of Jesus. He was not a miracle carnival, traveling around setting up his tent of miracles. He simply moved through life and responded to the needs that were present around him. Even though his calling was to destroy the works of the devil, he did not go on a crusade against darkness. He quietly moved in kingdom authority and responded when darkness manifested around him. Jesus simply lived out his calling with eyes alert to opportunities. He prayed and then commanded.

I regularly interact with people; I listen to their stories, and when brokenness is revealed, I ask them if I can pray for them. I am not a miracle worker, but I am an ambassador of the King. He has asked me to make space where his glory can be revealed. I cannot personally conjure up miracles, but I can make space for him to work through me, his ambassador. His job is the demonstration of the kingdom through signs and wonders. My job is to exercise faith and invite his intervention into the broken places of our world. I do this in private and in public prayer. I have never had a person turn prayer down. Of course this public prayer can sometimes get awkward, especially when I ask someone if I can pray for them and they immediately assume that the offer is a general offer to pray for them in the future. Then I put my hand on their shoulder and, with eyes open, invite God to touch that broken place of life. Again, I am just creating space for God.

What will happen if you begin doing this? People will be healed, relationships will be restored, demons will be cast away, jobs will be found, paths will be made straight, shalom will return, favor, identity recovery, salvation—the kingdom demonstrations that Jesus spoke of! But what if nothing happens? What if God does not heal? That is not my responsibility. God is responsible for that part of the equation. I am only responsible to take risks to create spaces for his kingdom to break-in. But if nothing happens, won't that move people further from God? I have actually found just the opposite. Sometimes people are simply moved that you cared enough to invoke God into the situation. And on the other side, I have prayed for people who immediately experienced intervention but it did not mean the person was restored in relationship to God. Miracles are not the cure-all. Miracles are an on-ramp to better kingdom delights.

If you want to see some of the ways that this has played out in my life, I encourage you to read my book *The Bold Christian*.[1] But do not wait for more training or for the right time to move in kingdom demonstration. In your new identity (as one Chosen), with your new assignment (as one Called), and with your full empowerment (as one Commissioned), take the risk of praying for God's intervention in the lives of people that you meet in the day-to-day.

25

COMMISSIONED: WHAT NEXT?

We are not chosen only to be recipients of grace but to be instruments of grace. The grace of God is expressed most profoundly in Jesus. He came to "seek and save" us. Once we experience being found, we are most alive when we hear his calling to go out and find the other not-yet-found ones. This call would be daunting except for the commission of the Lord. He sends us out equipped and empowered. We are not out there on our own.

I find that a lot of people in the contemporary church in America are bored. We have bought into an aspect of our culture—consumerism—that makes the church unhealthy. The church has spent a number of years trying to sell church by making church feel more welcoming and less "church-like." Though the intent was good, to eliminate some of the contextual blocks to faith, its application has proved incomplete. The new "followers" did not always grow in depth of faith, and eventually the consumers got bored with the newer "dumbed-down" version of faith and moved on to something else.

Jesus did not save us to be consumers. He saved us to be co-heirs and overcomers—Kingdom of God conquerors who advance by love, live in truth, and operate with power. Many people have become bored as recipients of grace because they have no outlet to be dispensers of grace. It is in the going out that we become alive. Whether pastoring in New Jersey or Connecticut, empowering leaders in France or Mali, or training leaders for the world, I have found that the people most alive are the ones fully engaged in the Restoration Project.

We are learning this lesson again with the 20- and 30-somethings of our area. They are not attracted to a religious event. I call this the church-as-entertainment-concert format. But they are inspired by being on mission. Inviting them to a slick church experience will not work. In fact, they prefer the ancient in spiritual matters, as opposed to the slick. But invite them to do social work with you on the broken aspects of the neighborhood and they are in.

The old model of Christendom was to invite wanderers into truth. After the message stuck, the church then discipled them to action in mission. The new missional model is to invite them on mission with well validated, authority-wielding, and Spirit-empowered Christ-followers. They will be discipled on the way to becoming Christ-followers.

Your sense of purpose will be ultimately found in being on mission!

NOW WHAT?

Get commissioned! Your commissioning begins with the King. Tim Keller uses a perfect image of how this happens. He reminds us that as Westerners we do not have a good sense of kingdom. Living in a democracy, we find the idea of having a sovereign reigning over us is a bit challenging. We cherish rights and self-expression. But at the very core of kingdom thinking is abandonment and surrender. In a kingdom, the servant-warrior walks into the king's chamber, lowers the head and bows the knee, lays his or her sword at the feet of the king, and declares "Command me!" Then the warrior is commissioned to go out and execute the king's desires. So it is in the kingdom of God. If you have not allowed the King to commission you, it is time to do so.[1]

Commissioning best happens in community—in the church. Don't think institution here. Think people! If you are not part of a church that is crossing boundaries with the gospel of the kingdom, then become a change agent. Lead the way. If after many efforts you are unsuccessful in leading a movement, find a group of Christ-followers with whom you can proactively be on mission. In the pattern of Barnabas and Paul, the call comes from the Holy Spirit, but it will be best executed in the community of the church.

Chosen, called, commissioned—if this were not enough—there is one more piece to give you courage: Celebrated!

PART FIVE

RESCUED FOR THE RESTORATION PROJECT: CELEBRATED AS OVERCOMERS

"IF YOU COULD DO ANYTHING—assuming that you had all you needed: resources, education, money, and time; and assuming you knew you were guaranteed success—what would you do?" This is a life-focus question, one that I have been asked when focusing on leadership development. It's a thought-provoking question. Rarely, though, does someone have all the resources in hand before chasing their calling. The question is still valid, however, because it can help us be sure that we are investing in our calling and vision for life, instead of simply existing. We are programmed to make a difference in our world. It is part of our creative DNA as created in the image of God.

I began this book by noting the questions that we want to answer: "Is my life making a difference?" or "Does my life really matter?" Because of the story that God is telling, the life that you are living matters immensely. And there is some more good news behind the story that God is telling: The Restoration Project is a guaranteed success.

I presently live in the world of finance. Before accepting the call to come to this unique community, I was uninformed of the intricacies of this world. I knew the basics: buy low, sell high; spend less than you make; be a good steward; honor God with the first fruits; and sacrifice to give. Now that I am a pastor in an area with a number of people working in the finance industry, I have learned a more nuanced perspective of those broad principles. I have also learned a whole new vocabulary from this world.

One of the acronyms I began hearing early upon my arrival into the area was expressed in a question—"What's your ROI?" What's your Return On Investment? ROI is really a stewardship declaration. ROI is what Jesus celebrated in the Parable of the Talents (Matthew 25:14-30). In the parable, a man of wealth was going on a journey, so he entrusted his property to his servants. On his return he went to the servants to find out their ROI. The two who doubled their initial endowment—the one who had been given two produced four and the one given five produced ten—received the commendation, "Well done, good and faithful servant." The one who played it safe and did not bring a return was rebuked in the parable. Return on Investment,

ROI can be applied to all areas of life. How am I investing my allotted time, talent, treasure, and the gospel message itself? The answer to that question will suggest a lot about my priorities.

The Restoration Project has the best and only **guaranteed** ROI in history. Why? The final result is already prophetically celebrated in the final chapter of the story that God is telling. Those chosen, called, and commissioned are celebrated in these final chapters of the story. Once again we need to get a biblical perspective if we are to remain fully engaged in the divine assignment. The next couple chapters will unfold the reality of the guarantee with implications to where we invest our lives right now.

26

APOCALYPSE THEN

THE APOCALYPSE OF JOHN, the book of Revelation, was written to encourage persecuted Christ-followers in the first century. Their declaration of Jesus as King did not land them in the best situation socially. We often forget that during the first four centuries of the Christian movement the Christ-followers were the underdogs—ostracized, marginalized, and often at risk of martyrdom. It would have been hard for them to see a positive ROI in their daily investment in living out their calling as the presence of Jesus in this world. Association with the name of Jesus meant more trouble to them than personal advance.

In our contemporary world, when we hear the word *apocalypse*, we think of extensive destruction of the sort portrayed in films that bear that name. *Apocalypse* actually meant *unveiling* in the original language. God was pulling the curtain back for the people to see the actual outcome of their lives. Their ROI was actually quite impressive. The Lord left these early, endangered Christ-followers this final word through the prophetic visions of John the Apostle so that they would not lose hope.

In Revelation my favorite images of the final results are the throne scenes in heaven. Jesus takes his place on the throne and the throngs break into worship. Let the following passage tell the story. Take time to read it slowly; even read it a second time to discover the underlying statements that intersect with what we have already discussed about God's Mission and the Restoration Project.

> Then I saw in the right hand of him who was seated on the throne a scroll written within and on the back, sealed with seven seals. And I saw a mighty angel proclaiming with a loud voice, "Who is worthy to open the scroll and break its seals?" And no one in heaven or on earth or under the earth was able to open the scroll or to look into it, and I began to weep loudly because no one was found worthy to open the scroll or to look into it. And one of the elders said to me, "Weep no more; behold, the Lion of the tribe of Judah, the Root of David, has conquered, so that he can open the scroll and its seven seals."
> And between the throne and the four living creatures and among the elders I saw a Lamb standing, as though it had been slain, with seven horns and with seven eyes, which are the

seven spirits of God sent out into all the earth. And he went and took the scroll from the right hand of him who was seated on the throne. And when he had taken the scroll, the four living creatures and the twenty-four elders fell down before the Lamb, each holding a harp, and golden bowls full of incense, which are the prayers of the saints. And they sang a new song, saying,

"Worthy are you to take the scroll
and to open its seals,
for you were slain, and by your blood you ransomed people for
 God
from every tribe and language and people and nation,
and you have made them a kingdom and priests to our God,
and they shall reign on the earth."

Then I looked, and I heard around the throne and the living
 creatures and the elders the voice of many angels, numbering
 myriads of myriads and thousands of thousands, saying with
 a loud voice,
"Worthy is the Lamb who was slain,
to receive power and wealth and wisdom and might
and honor and glory and blessing!"

And I heard every creature in heaven and on earth and under
 the earth and in the sea, and all that is in them, saying,
"To him who sits on the throne and to the Lamb
be blessing and honor and glory and might forever and ever!"

And the four living creatures said, "Amen!" and the elders fell down and worshiped (Revelation 5).

The visual images of these prophecies are quite graphic. The heavenly scene begins with a period of anticipation, waiting for the celebration of the redemption of humanity. It is waiting for the culmination of history. The groan of creation heard in Romans 8—awaiting eagerly for the adoption as sons—echoes here in Revelation 5 in the heavenly throne room. Who will bring the wait of history to consummation?

Finally, Jesus, the Lion of Judah and the Lamb who was slain, steps forward to break open the scroll, which sets off a worship celebration. In the first wave of worship the worth of Jesus is declared because he has "ransomed people for God from every tribe, language, people, and nation, and he made them a kingdom and priests to our God, to reign on the earth" (5:9-10).

Ransomed—bought out slavery—Rescued.

Reigning—the kingdom restored—Restoration Project.

After these images of worship, the Revelation then goes on to describe what this Restoration entails. Revelation 7 describes the abolition of hunger, thirst, and oppression, as God leads his people to springs of living water and wipes away every tear (Revelation 7:15-17). Revelation 12 and 20 describe the complete defeat of darkness. I want to remind us at this point that this was a far reality to what the people were experiencing in John's day. They were physically hungry, thirsty, and oppressed as a result of following Jesus. It felt at times like darkness was winning.

Fast-forward to our day, twenty centuries later, and the situation of Christ followers looks far different, at least in our part of the world. Even so, the promises of Restoration still feel far off.

So the anticipation felt so palpably in the heavenly throne room before the opening of the scrolls is still with us. It is the longing within us that has led us to declare, "There has to be more to life" each time we face all the brokenness and futility around us. There *is* more to life. The *not yet* aspect of the kingdom is waiting for consummation.

Throughout the Revelation to John, the Restoration images build to a climax, and. in the final chapter of Revelation, God reveals the final chapter of his story:

> *Then the angel showed me the river of the water of life, bright as crystal, flowing from the throne of God and of the Lamb through the middle of the street of the city; also, on either side of the river, the tree of life with its twelve kinds of fruit, yielding its fruit each month. The leaves of the tree were for the healing of the nations. No longer will there be anything accursed, but the throne of God and of the Lamb will be in it, and his servants will worship him. They will see his face, and his name will be on their foreheads. And night will be no more. They will need no light of lamp or sun, for the Lord God will be their light, and they will reign forever and ever* (Revelation 22:1-5).

What had been marred at the Fall will be completely Restored. The state of brokenness and all of the effects of the Fall will be overcome—COMPLETELY! Our investment in that Restoration will be rewarded. What began in a garden moves to a city, and ends in a mixed metaphor where city-street and flowing river come together. Creation no longer groans but intersects perfectly with humanity to reflect the glory of God.

This whole paragraph is celebratory, but one phrase captures my attention in light of the Larger Story that God is telling—**the healing of the nations.**

The language here ties together the entire biblical record. What was promised to Abram (Genesis 12), commissioned through Moses (Exodus 19), revealed in Jonah, made possible in Jesus, and re-commissioned through the church (I Peter 2), this is what is being realized in the end times. These prophetic images of the glorification of Jesus, the Lamb who was slain, express the end result for humanity—the gathering of the peoples and nations into vibrant worship of God.

Simply put, we get an advance picture of the success of the Restoration Project. Paradise restored. Guaranteed by God and His Word! This is especially important in light of John's original audience. Everything about their situation, when viewed through human eyes and minds, did not declare victory, so this promise of eventual victory meant everything to them and gave them the courage to persevere. And the promises of those prophetic images flow forward to encourage us today, we who are the followers of Christ and advancers of his kingdom. These images of victory might not mean so much to people who live in comfort or ease. However, to those overcoming the brokenness of their own personal world and to those who have chosen to enter the brokenness of the world of others by engaging in the Restoration Project, these are the best images possible. They give hope and the strength to persevere.

Humankind was created to be a reflection of God's glory: we are invited to express his glory as we participate in the tasks of co-creation, ruling, and living out the perfected fellowship that Father, Son, and Holy Spirit share in eternity. The book of Revelation is the picture of the Restoration of this original design. Missions are only necessary to reunite the dispersed nations to the original design. John Piper captures this notion in a brilliant description:

> Missions are not the ultimate goal of the church. Worship is. Missions exist because worship doesn't. Worship is ultimate, not missions, because God is ultimate, not man. When this age is over, and the countless millions of the redeemed fall on their faces before the throne of God, missions will be no more. It is a temporary necessity. But worship abides forever.
>
> Worship, therefore, is the fuel and goal of missions. It's the goal of missions because in missions we simply aim to bring the nations into white-hot enjoyment of God's glory.[1]

This was the long declared expectation: "May the peoples praise you, O God; may all the peoples praise you! May the nations *be glad and sing for joy!*" (Psalm 67:3-4).

During this in-between time, as we wait for the final pages of the story, the Restoration Project is being carried out by people on mission—the church active as the agent doing missions. It is at this time, when we are living for the glory of Jesus and working toward the honor of his name, that we are most alive. And it is when humanity is restored in relationship to him that God is most glorified.

Revelation, the final chapter of the story that God is telling, guarantees victory. It guarantees the best return on our investment of our lives. This promise is as important to us today as it was to the earliest followers. The next chapter will unpack more of our present longing in anticipation of the paradise restored.

27

LONGING NOW: THIS CANNOT BE ALL THERE IS!

WHY IS THIS IMAGE OF FINAL RESTORATION so important? Whether we realize it or not, we all have in our hearts this same longing for and expectation of Restoration. We cannot help but see the brokenness all around us. We experience it in our own lives. We read and hear about it in the news. Our world is a mess. The declaration of Historical Determinism, which stated that in history we are naturally progressing toward utopia, keeps tripping over the realities of our world. And we have this nagging sense that we were made for a different story. I think this is why the epic narratives of good winning over evil are still the biggest box office draws in the theatre. They are echoing the story that God is telling.

I once heard Ravi Zacharias preach a sermon entitled "Why the Fairytale Writers Get It Right When the Philosophers Get It Wrong." His premise was that contemporary philosophers have arrived at meaninglessness and ultimate nihilism, whereas the fairytales end with Right winning the day. The promise of Restoration, of Right winning the day, stands against many of our life experiences in which Right does not win. Though the Christian movement has radically advanced since the days when the letter of Revelation was originally penned to the church, we still know of many people who are still distant to their creator and live in misery and fear.

For example, today I observed this brokenness all around me. As I ordered coffee at a coffee shop, the woman working behind the counter hustled to be a good server. She worked diligently to bring order to the chaos of people trying to get their orders quickly. She was being pleasant to not-so-pleasant customers. But at the same time there were signs of disorder written on her countenance. Her eyes emitted sadness. She projected a lack of self-confidence even as she served even through the performed outward pleasantness. I wondered about her story. What type of chaos was she dealing with at home? What were her dreams? Was she aware of where her story fit in God's story? Would an understanding of that truth change everything about the struggle she felt in the every day?

That young woman was just one of hundreds of people with whom I crossed paths today. How about the many people that I know more closely who face what may feel like insurmountable circumstances—broken bodies, broken souls, and broken relationships, which lead to broken dreams and broken hope? The suffering for some of these people may not be intense right now, but for some suffering has been their daily experience for many years. And this is just the situation close to my everyday reality.

How about the suffering that extends out to the extremities of the world, a world that I primarily hear about in news reports? The list of broken circumstances is reported daily in the broadcasts that I watch: wars, famines, terrorism, displacement, trafficking, epidemics, lack of work opportunities, unavailable clean water, and hosts of broken relationships.

And, if all of this were not enough, for those of us who live what appear to be outwardly blessed lives, there is still a dull sense at our core that we limp through life as strangers and aliens to this world. Even the most optimistic of us have to look at our world and declare, "It is severely broken!"

One of my friends is a psychiatrist and he lovingly calls me a "Psycho Utopian." I am always disappointed when people do not get along or cooperate. I would like to have just one day when even the people of God got along—no petty comparisons, no cynicism, no gossip—to simply be the family of God together on mission to address the brokenness of our world rather than together reproducing hurt within the family. Just one day! Why is that desire there? I think it is the longing for the Kingdom that has not yet fully arrived—the final chapter of the Restoration Project.

I think what makes the longing so strong is that we have tasted the "kingdom now" that Jesus announced and demonstrated. I have seen immediate on-the-spot healings, events that can only be explained as divine interventions. I have seen lives radically turned around—Rescue. I have seen neighborhoods brought from absolute chaos to a semblance of order—Restoration. All of these spaces of transformation have been God-saturated moments where the kingdom overcame the results of the Fall. But we still live with the tension of the "kingdom not yet" that Jesus promised. We have a foretaste in our partial experiences now, but brokenness still faces us daily. The nibble on "the now" makes the full banquet of the "not yet" so much more palpable. Heaven—paradise lost. The distant echo is in our *imago dei* saturated imaginations.

There will always be an echo of more coming until Jesus returns and makes all things new. It is what we pray for every day or at least what we pray for in our worship gatherings every week: "Your Kingdom come and Your Will be done on earth as it is in heaven." It is the longing of all, but especially of the people of God. Lord, Ephesians 3:20 us: do more than we could ever ask or imagine! Lord, Revelation 21 us: heal the nations! And in so doing, glorify Jesus through white-hot worship from the nations!!

Given the hurt and pain that we face every day, our own and that of our acquaintances and friends, we could easily lose hope. But the promise drives us. The hard part is that there is often a long lag time between the promise, calling, and vision, and the fulfillment of all the above. In fact, we might never see the promises fulfilled in our own lifetime. Hebrews 11 is referred to as the great chapter of faith. It lists many of the people who with faith overcame overwhelming circumstances. As noted earlier, some of those people are household names and others are unnamed. These faith heroes are linked together by two common factors. First, they faced incredible opposition in life. Secondly, "by faith" they took on those obstacles—some overcoming in incredible victory and some probably disappointed with the earthly result of their faith. But in the end, both the overcomers and the disappointed were not expressing hope and living in faith just for themselves. They were part of a bigger story. Two times in the faith chapter it is said of them that they "did not receive what was promised." Interestingly, it is said of both those who experienced "victory" in the temporal and those who did not get what they wanted; each did not fully receive what was promised.

What does that phrase mean—they didn't get what was promised? What were they promised? Was Jesus what they hoped for? Yes. The Messianic expectation drove the people who are celebrated in Hebrews 11. However, it was not just the appearance of the Messiah they awaited, but the accompanying Messianic rule they hoped for. The text itself points to this longing. They longed for Restoration:

> "These all died in faith, not having received the things promised, but having seen them and greeted them from afar, and having acknowledged that they were strangers and exiles on the earth. For people who speak thus make it clear that they are seeking a homeland. If they had been thinking of that land from which they had gone out, they would have had opportunity to return. But as it is, they desire a better country, that is, a heavenly one. Therefore God is not ashamed to be called their God, for he has prepared for them a city" (Hebrews 11:13-16).

They knew that this world was not the ultimate. They were strangers, exiles, and pilgrims passing through. They were seeking a better patronage, a Kingdom that really works according to the original design. A city that God had prepared, with a river running through and trees that bore leaves for the healing of the nations! They waited for the promise to be fulfilled. The writer of Hebrews completes the chapter with a reminder that we carry on the task of holding out in hope for the promises not yet realized: "that apart from us they should not be made perfect" (Hebrews 11:40). Jesus waits for his enemies to be made his footstool and the great cloud of saints who embraced this vision and who persevered in faith wait for us to fulfill our assignments in the Restoration Project.

And so the declaration to God's people was always to persevere in the face of opposition. The next chapter, Hebrews 12, calls us to throw off everything that weighs us down, so that we can run our leg of the race. Our motivation is the example of Jesus who endured the cross "for the joy set before him" (12:2). It was never declared to be easy. That is why in God's Word we are called soldiers, co-laborers, wrestlers, and overcomers. Each calling implies hard work and struggle, but our effort comes with a guaranteed promise of success. In Galatians 6:9, Paul declares it to be so: "and let us not grow weary in doing good, for in due season we will reap, if we do not give up."

Revelation—the image of the Restoration Project completed—becomes motivation to continue on in the face of opposition. We need to celebrate what is already celebrated in Holy Writ. Jesus is the glorious King and we, the Jesus followers, will overcome by the blood of the Lamb and by our testimony.

28

CELEBRATED THEN: LIVE INTO YOUR FINAL DESTINY NOW

FOUR BIG THEMES—Creation, Fall, Rescue, Restoration. The Story begins with God and the Story ends with God. We are most alive when we see how our stories intersect with his Story. I personally do not want to wait for this to just happen to me; I want the take hold of it, to seize my creative purpose. Finding this intersection of our stories with his story is an expression of a common need of all humans. We long to have significance.

I return to the earlier question: "Does my life really matter?"

That longing for purposeful living is rooted in our creative design. Created in God's image—a God who is purposeful, who brings order out of chaos, a God on mission—created in the image of this God we are naturally given to purposefulness. Fall mars the purposefulness and adds strife to the fulfillment, but the longing for purpose is still there. Enter Jesus—Rescuer and commissioner to Restoration, and our longing becomes even greater because we get a taste of the Kingdom come. And we hold on to this until it is completely revealed, knowing the end result is guaranteed—even if we do not see it in our own lives.

Some people feel that the task is so great that they cannot see themselves as having any significance in the Story that God is telling. I have had people say to me, "God has more important things to do than be alert to my prayers." Others feel that their lives are too ordinary or too broken to be used. Consider the characters that Jesus used in recorded biblical history. I have read on many websites the following description of some of them (original source unknown):

> Jacob was a cheater, Peter had a temper, David had an affair, Noah got drunk, Jonah ran from God, Paul was a murderer, Gideon was insecure, Miriam was a gossiper, Martha was a worrier, Thomas was a doubter, Sara was impatient, Elijah was moody, Moses stuttered, Zaccheus was short, Abraham was old, and Lazarus was dead… God doesn't call the qualified; He qualifies the CALLED!

Your story does matter in the story that God is telling. You too have a part. And it is a victorious part!

Your embracing this reality is not just for you. This is not self-realization psychotherapy. It is about the glory of Jesus. It is about the not-yet-rescued people and the not-yet-restored nations. As the rescued and being restored ones, we are the hope bearers for a world that needs hope. The Psalmist repeatedly declares this anticipation: *I wait for the Lord.* What is the object of this hope? God. The people of God do not hope *for* something as much as they hope *in* something, or rather in someone: God. We are the ones who point to a God who wills and works good for his creation, calling it from brokenness to restoration. He is the God who works in partnership, and so we step up to this calling with all of his resources. And we do not lose hope because the victory is guaranteed in the final chapters of the God Story.

So what is my next step? Get to it! Be proactive! Don't let your story happen to you. Be an active voice in the telling of God's narrative through you. Live on purpose. Please understand, I am not talking about Messiah-complex living, or striving to earn favor with God. I am talking about abiding in Jesus to continue his mission in this world: partnership in the Restoration Project.

Jesus says it so clearly in his teaching in John 15. He uses the image of the vine and branches. He reminds us as his followers that we were meant to bear fruit. This reminder comes with a promise of success: "whoever abides in me and I in him, will bear much fruit" (John 15:5). God is glorified when we "bear much fruit" (15:8). The image is a perfect restraint to self-initiation. Branches are only conduits of the nutrients that come from the vine. Branches do nothing on their own. What is their task? To abide. To stay connected. We simply need to stay connected to Jesus and watch what he does through our attentive lives.

In the end, it is not so much about getting to the right place or finding the right assignment or developing the purposeful plan and purpose-filled life. It is about being attentive to what God is doing in the world and in the circumstances where we presently find ourselves. In that attentiveness, he will direct us in how we should go, what we should do, and even what we should say. Then one day we will turn around and declare, ***What an amazing journey God has led me on!*** Then the following day we will be part of that great throng of worshippers who celebrate the glory of the Lamb.

> *"Worthy is the Lamb who was slain, to receive power and wealth*
> *and wisdom and might and honor and glory and blessing!"*
> (Revelation 5:12).

29

CONTEMPORARY STORIES: PEOPLE PURPOSEFUL IN THE RESTORATION PROJECT

LIFE IS A STORY and it unfolds as drama, comedy, tragedy, love story, and mystery, all in one. G.K. Chesterton notes, "I had always felt life first as a story; and if there is a story there is a story-teller."[1] My simple point for this book is that God is the ultimate Storyteller. Life is not an exercise in the endurance of randomness. There is a plot. We are the characters of God's choosing to tell the story, characters who act and who make choices. We are not simply robots or puppets in this Story.

There is a mystery to this interplay between the sovereignty of God and the freewill he has assigned to the characters in his story. The script is not rigid, yet the drama continues to move to the grand final act. Thus we are invited to find our roles in the grand design.

Since life is a story, maybe the way God mysteriously works through people is best expressed in story. We began this journey by entering more deeply into the story of one man: Jonah. He becomes for us a metaphor of God's purpose in the lives of all of his children. The rest of the Bible is filled with stories of people who played significant roles in the God Story. We observed that some roles are public and prominent, while others are unseen, and yet are they just as prominent. Thus, to bring this book full circle, it is best to tell the stories of contemporary people who have proactively lived their stories in light of God's larger narrative.

All these stories are precious to me because they represent people with whom God has given me the privilege of sharing this life journey. I have changed the names to keep from embarrassing them, but the stories are true. They are ordinary people like you and I. I could tell stories of missionaries with whom I have rubbed shoulders. I could point out Christian leaders who are public figures for the Kingdom of God. However, I choose to here focus in on a few people who will never be recognized in national magazines or in chronicles of church history. Yet each of these people is making a significant difference in the Restoration Project. The purpose in telling their stories is to inspire sanctified imagination in the discovery of our own callings and roles in the Story that God is telling.

JEREMY

Jeremy was a teacher and a baseball coach. He was living the normal American life. He worked hard, he made a living, he raised kids—basically, he did life. Jeremy knew God and was doing his best to serve the Christian community in a youth ministry. Though this was honorable, and was maybe even the role he was meant to play at that point in his story, some things happened to disrupt the story line. He made a bad choice and almost destroyed his marriage. He then experienced rescue a second time and began the work of personal restoration. That work required grace, forgiveness, worship, service, going deeper in the Word, and time. In the process, God solidified Jeremy's identity—it was situated in Christ, not in his own performance. God restored his marriage. After some time, God gave Jeremy his ultimate assignment: he was called to cross boundaries to carry God's love to the marginalized of this world.

How did Jeremy get to this place of calling? One day he decided that he had studied God's Word so long that it was time to do the "stuff" found in the stories of the Book, to become involved in the real plot behind the Big Story. Parts of that God-preserved story came alive as he read the Bible through the lens of Jesus's parable of the Good Samaritan. Then one day he read *The Hole in Our Gospel* by Richard Stearns. A couple sentences in Stearn's book seemed to become Jeremy's driving force:

> And if Jesus was willing to die for this troubled planet, maybe I need to care about it too…being a Christian, or follower of Jesus Christ, requires more than just having a personal and transforming relationship with God. It also entails a public and transforming relationship with the world.[2]

Jeremy was hooked. Holy discontent took over. It began with efforts to serve food and deliver clothes to the homeless in his own "backyard," in communities not far from where he lived. He mentored troubled youth. He rebuilt broken spaces. He invested in others for rescue and restoration. He himself had known failure, so he knew there was no one beyond his love investment. He would show them the same unconditional love that he had experienced from God, love that led to his own restoration. In doing so, he desired to lead them to restoration in God. Jeremy's passion stretched beyond the local to international places of poverty, where he could be God's hands of love. He did this while he continued to fulfill his responsibilities at work. He cared for people at work too, modeling God's love for them and, when appropriate, speaking to them of that love.

For Jeremy, his time was a gift from God and it was to be stewarded well. God owned all of his time and so the mission of God (*missio Dei*) became his mission. His vocation became God saturated. His avocation and free time also became God saturated through service. Then Jeremy went from being a doer of mission to becoming a mobilizer of others. He called fellow Christ-followers to join the effort. He organized the collection of resources to respond to disasters. He tirelessly gave of his time to model the way for others. Quite simply, he played his role according to the larger script. He was blessed to be a blessing. And he called the other blessed to do the same.

Now Jeremy could have played it safe and lived more comfortably over these past few years. He took risks for the sake of God. When he retired from his first vocation, teaching, he asked the Lord to release him to his second calling, previously his avocation. Today he is a tireless ambassador of God's love. And his efforts are multiplied because he rarely does this work alone. Jeremy is constantly inviting, prodding, organizing, exhorting, and partnering with other ambassadors so that they can discover their new assignment in the Restoration Project. He is part of a faith community that is changing the world, and Jeremy is a major player in that effort. Blessed to be a blessing

BILL AND PATTY

From all external observations, Bill and Patty have it made. They live in the land of comfort and their life together is marked by opportunity. Probably ninety percent of the world's population would trade positions with them in a moment. However, their life situation has not always been so outwardly blessed. They have walked through some years of pain. Patty survived a bad marriage and divorce, and the resulting relational and emotional pain that accompanies the rupture of covenant. Bill's life too was riddled with the pain of a broken marriage. But God is the God of rescue and restoration. Part of their restoration was a second opportunity at marriage, with each other.

Bill was immersed in God's Story daily, and he prayed it into his own life and the lives of others. Thus, their new opportunity in marriage was rooted in the foundation of the Larger Story that God was telling. Their union became established on the foundation of the Word. Both Bill and Patty found places to serve within the church. However, it did not take long for their sanctified imaginations to be captured by God's Mission in this world. Together they stewarded their second chance by going full force into the Restoration Project.

They had the means to financially empower a number of efforts. They did not shy away from being generous. She had the leadership ability to mobilize efforts to change the world for others. She was a tireless volunteer, using her gifts for the benefit of others. He was strategic in his contribution to the boards of organizations that were making a difference in reaching the world. Not only did they give financially, they multiplied their impact by inviting others to give sacrificially as well. And the giving of their wealth was just the beginning of their steward-ship. They then began finding ways to invest themselves through volunteerism. They were stewarding their time and talents, as well as their treasure.

Together they became exposed to the world on the other side of the tracks: broken neighborhoods and broken lives in America, orphanages in Africa, AIDS clinics in India, interna-tional educational institutes giving opportunities to those who would normally be without opportunity. They crossed bound-aries to engage the poor, entering into their world to touch their pain, and to have relationship in order to add to the dignity of the lives of the marginalized.

Bill and Patty could easily have sat back and enjoyed the benefits of having made it to a place of financial comfort. However, this couple is making a difference in our world through fully living God's Story. Blessed to be a blessing!

FRED

Fred was a man on the rise. Powerful job. Beautiful family. Big house. But, as in many stories of privilege, a focus on self can lead to destruction. It all came apart. The marriage ended bit-terly. The power job disappeared, and the big house and life perks were gone shortly thereafter. Fred became dependent on the charity of others. Desperate, at the end of his rope, Fred was rescued. He knew about God before the rescue, but it was through the faithful witness of the Christ community that he came to personally know God through Jesus Christ. He got absorbed into that faith community, and he saturated himself in God's Word. Prayer became his life source. The combination of God's Word, prayer, and Christian community began a process of transformation—the Holy Spirit likes to land here at the intersection of the Word, prayer, and community.

I wish I could say everything turned around right away for Fred. There were God interventions, but for Fred it always felt like he was standing on one new precipice after another, relationally or financially. Then, to top things off, he almost died. All the miracles of his life in that period seem too crazy to be true. But the Story God is telling is a bit crazy too. When Fred did recover, he wanted to give back. He was aware that not only had he been given new life in Christ, he had also literally been given a second physical life. He initially gave back by serving the people of God. Fred's desire to serve, though, went beyond the people of God. He made himself available at every turn.

All his personal desires did not, as a result, come into fruition, but there were signs of changes in the future that gave him hope. His identity was being restored. In his previous life, Fred had always been able to make things happen. He was— and still is—a leader and mobilizer. He was conditioned by the American dream: if he just did enough, worked the angles, leveraged his relationships, he could get anything done. Then God gave him a God-sized assignment. Fred was called to be part of the Restoration Project in an impossible international situation. His start at fulfilling this assignment was noble and rightly motivated. But there was still that underlying philosophy to his life: if *he* did enough, he could accomplish the job: he could rescue a bunch of marginalized kids in the majority world.

Then he had to learn the final lesson. He was not able to help these kids, but God was able. God used a recovering identity, along with an impossible assignment, to give Fred his greatest fulfillment in life to date. He is playing his role according to God's script now, abiding and not striving; and the miracles of God's intervention are flowing through him for the blessing of others.

Does Fred have it all worked out? Absolutely not. Are there still personal and family dreams that lie in the back of his sanctified imagination? Absolutely. But today Fred is alive in the deepest sense—spiritually—because he is reconnected to his true identity in Christ and to his life assignment. Blessed to be a blessing!

LUCY

Lucy has had a pretty uneventful life so far. She had not been a rebellious teen. She followed her parents' teachings and, for whatever reason, she found it easy to follow Jesus. The things of this world did not really draw her in. She has lived out of the common and saving grace of God most of her life. As a result, she doesn't have any great stories of recovery. She married her university love. They had children early. They had made a decision early in their marriage not to over-extend themselves financially to ensure that she would not have to work outside the home. Her vocation was to provide a nourishing household for the benefit of her family. Her first calling was to invest in her kingdom family.

Lucy does not have a lot of time for herself. However, she

does not mind this; in fact, she has embraced this calling from God. Her goal, though, is different than the goals of many people in her sphere of influence. She is not working to make her kids famous or successful. She lives for them to love God and love their neighbors as themselves. She makes every effort to put God first in the equations of life. Time is invested with God in mind. Getting-to-know-God goals are as important as other developmental goals for her children. Serving people is programmed into the family's weekly schedule so that it becomes the norm for her children. She is invested in creating Kingdom kids.

Lucy is working toward legacy. She is not just existing; she is living on purpose. When it fits into their schedule, she volunteers to serve in ministries at church and in the community. She especially likes behind-the-scenes efforts where her service can do the talking for her. The outside world will not recognize her as significant, yet she is a chosen, called, and commissioned ambassador to that world. The result of her investment will be a generation of world changers. She will one day be celebrated when it matters most and by whom it matters most.

There is one other aspect of Lucy's life where she is highly engaged in the Restoration Project. She has come into contact with a number of people on mission in the world. Traditionally they have been called missionaries, though more recently her contacts have been those living in places where it would be dangerous for missionaries to live so they perform their mission through different vocations. Every morning, when the last child is off to school, she has a three-hour window for herself. Household chores take up most of that time, but she is vigilant to guard an hour of quietness. She reads God's Word, journals, and intercedes for those international workers. She is part of their story as they live out their calling to be God's love in places that she will never visit. In those moments, life stories get intertwined in the Larger Story that God is telling. Lucy is part of the power source and support for a number of people on mission who are bringing the Restoration Project to some of the most desperate corners of our globe. Blessed to be a blessing.

QUICK GLIMPSES AT OTHER EXAMPLES OF INVESTMENT IN THE RESTORATION PROJECT

Mary has situated her interior design business to help people invest their pre-owned furniture in the lives of marginalized urbanites. Will organizes the food preparation for a homeless shelter in the next town. Tim hosts an event at his home to introduce local people beyond the faith community to ministries that care for people who survive in some of the most dangerous slums in the world. Sally takes her teens to a social center one afternoon per week to offer mentoring for less fortunate children. Ferdinand and Magna adopted five children from an impoverished area of our world, rescuing children abandoned into an orphanage. Tom and Grace, along with their three children, spend one Sunday afternoon per month at a dormitory for troubled children. Susan rallies a group of teens each year to Christmas carol at homes of shut-ins and at the local senior care centers. Faith organizes the preparation of nine hundred sandwiches after a church service. These sandwiches will feed for a week a neighborhood of children in a troubled area; many of these kids would not have lunch without this assistance. Bill, working in a high-stress finance office, lives with such hope that he is regularly approached for counsel and prayer, through which he becomes a witness for Christ. Dave serves on the local school board to be a presence of the Kingdom in the community. MaryJo serves in a church plant each week in an urban setting. Her desire would be to worship at the main campus of her church where she has been in community for years. However, she is choosing this small sacrifice of comfort to see the gospel spread into a new area. And the list goes on. Each person is making a difference in our world as an active player in the Restoration Project. Blessed to be a blessing!

I could tell dozens of other stories of ordinary people who have agreed to partner with an extraordinary God. Included in those stories are some amazing God-orchestrated moments of calling and direction. Mixed in the storylines are some not-so-wonderful failures and disappointing turns. But the consistent theme in each is the intertwining of smaller stories into God's Bigger Story. After Rescue in Jesus comes Restoration with Jesus. The invitation to Restoration is the invitation to allow our path to join the larger narrative of God. J.R.R. Tolkien says it well through the voice of Bilbo in Rivendell after the hobbits have returned from their journey:

> *The Road goes ever on and on*
> *Down from the door where it began.*
> *Now far ahead the Road has gone,*
> *And I must follow, if I can,*
> *Pursuing it with eager feet,*
> *Until it joins some larger way . . .* [3]

C.S. Lewis, an avid letter writer, also wrote of this story and this road. Many of these letters of his are recorded in a book entitled *Yours, Jack*. Reading through the progression of his own faith journey is an experience that inspires my own growth. In a letter written on 5 February 1954, he makes the following statement:

> "How little they know of Christianity who think that the story ends with conversion; novelties we never dreamed of may await us at every turn of the road."[4]

What I have discovered in my own journey is that some of those novelties are interlaced with my engagement in the Restoration Project. My world has expanded by crossing boundaries in Jesus's name. With identity recovered and assignment embraced, life takes on real meaning and purpose.

Your life matters! Play the role that God has designed for you!!

APPENDIX ONE

A MODEL OF REFLECTION

THROUGHOUT HISTORY, the Christian faith has had a tradition of proactive listening in order to discern God's will for individuals and communities. We see this modeled in the New Testament church at Antioch in Acts 13. It was during a time of fasting and prayer that the church heard the Holy Spirit's direction to set apart Barnabas and Saul as missionaries. The key to this process is often a time of retreat, a stepping aside from the regular flow of life to create space for listening. I do not believe that this is merely an individualistic pursuit; it happens best in community. Any insights that one receives need to be confirmed in the faith community, where accountability and correction can help can keep a calling on target. However, the process can be initiated by an individual and then later brought into a mutual space of listening to trusted journeyers in faith. The following exercise will give you some reflective tools to think about potential callings that God has been shaping in your life.

Set aside a morning or afternoon when you can find some time of quietness and reflection. Go off to a place of solitude, where the noises of life have less pull on your attention (much as Jesus did when he wanted direction from the Father). Invite God into that space, and walk through the following steps during this reflection period. If you are a person who likes to know the complete map, read through the descriptions of the steps below before beginning, in order to get a sense of the process. Otherwise, you can read the description of each stage, one at a time while engaging with the model. See the model below. I offer a number of examples from my own life as illustrations to unlock your sanctified imagination.

STEP 1

Begin by taking a memory journey through your life, recalling moments where you experienced success. It may have been a moment you experienced satisfaction or a time your success was confirmed through the words of another person. Attempt to narrow the reflection chronologically through life stages or blocks of time. After you have taken a full lifespan view, you may find it useful to go back into each example of success at a later time to add nuances to the insights that you have gained.

After you have followed through each stage, take a bird's-eye view to see if there are any patterns that repeat in each stage.

In doing so, you will be bringing some life competencies to the surface. Then attempt to summarize what you see as your life contribution or investment of giftedness and personhood. Arthur Miller calls this your Motivated Abilities Pattern (MAP). I highly recommend his book *The Power of Uniqueness*[1] as a tool to take this review deeper at a later time.

To give you an example, when I went through this process I discovered that my MAP was as a "Collaborative, Catalyzing Prime Mover and Enabler of Growth." Throughout my life, even though I am at core an introvert, I have been thrust into spaces where I was charged to lead a group to a preferred future. As I reviewed my life with the guidance of a life coach, it became clear that I am most alive when I use my gifts and passions to inspire a group of people to have faith in moving toward a God-sized vision.

STEP 2

Note what you have learned about yourself from personality and behavioral assessment tests that you have completed in the past. The list of assessment tools is large and includes the Meyers-Briggs Type Indicator, DiSC Profile and Spiritual Gifts Inventory, The Birkman Method, Keirsey Temperament Sorter, 16PF Test, Leadership Skills Assessment Tool, Management by Strengths, and IDAK Career Assessment. If you have, in the past, taken any of these tests or tests like them, this would be a good time to take out those results and look over them again to remind yourself of your strengths.

If you haven't yet taken such tests, consider doing it later and then coming back through the exercise incorporating what new insights you have gained. The information gained can help you see more clearly your God-given and socially learned assets to be used for his glory. I have taken two new assessment tests in the past three months and I have found them helpful in shaping my leadership role in the Restoration Project. The more you see, the more you know; and the more you know, the more you will see.

It is always important to remember that these tests are descriptive, not prescriptive. Some people become a bit afraid of such assessments as they view them as limiting. A discovery of a tendency does not mean that it needs to become a label that defines a person. If we take the results as prescriptive, they can be limiting. But if we receive the results as descriptive, they can be aligning.

These assessments can be revealing. They are designed to recognize when we are giving an incongruent set of answers or when we are presenting our ideal world as opposed to our real life experience. In this way, their objective feedback can be eye opening. It can also be confirming, helping us focus our effort in our places of strength and calling. If you have not completed any assessments, they are available online.

I personally have found Meyers-Briggs and the DiSC Profile and Spiritual Gifts Inventory to be the most insightful. The value of the DiSC profile is that it reveals where our behavioral reflex response impacts people with different profiles. I am a High D/I on the DiSC profile. Without getting into the details, it means I can be a scary leader for people with a C/S profile, and that is important for me to know. This impacts my communication style and processing of team dynamics. As a visionary leader, with dominant gifts of faith and leadership, and with a leadership style that would be described as inspirational or motivational, I need C/S people around me to be successful.

Knowing the behavioral reflex response of my team members gives me insight on how to create team space and communicate for a greater synergy of impact of the team.

These assessments are also important for guarding my emotional health as a leader. I am an Introvert on the Meyers-Briggs PT. How does a high D/I, with motivational gifts and style survive as an Introvert? I must be purposeful in finding space apart for my own refueling to keep me in a state of wellbeing to fulfill my many corporate responsibilities.

STEP 3

List your four primary spiritual gifts. You can also take a spiritual gifts test online. I recommend finding a spiritual gifts test that is linked to the DiSC profile. The DiSC profile will give nuanced understanding of the manifestation of your spiritual gifts. You can do an internet search of "DiSC and Spiritual Gifts" to find this free resource.

I encourage you to list your three or four highest scored gifts because I have observed that people often have a gift cluster that becomes their sweet spot for doing ministry. Other gifts will ebb and flow as needed for certain situations. However, I believe we all have our sweet spot of contribution through the primary grace endowments that the Holy Spirit has chosen to give us.

When looking at my primary manifestation of spiritual gifts from the list found in Ephesians 4, I come up strong as an apostolic teacher. I do serve at times in the roles of pastor, evangelist, and prophet, but these are not my strongest places of engagement. Because my vocation at this time is as a pastor, much of my life is given to pastoring. With an apostolic bent (a sent one, one who likes to cross boundaries, a creative entrepreneur, missionary) and as a witness, I do evangelism. As a communicator or discerner of spirits, I will receive prophetic utterances. However, I am most alive when communicating for the purpose of mobilizing a people for change, transformation, and making a difference in this world.

When I add my cluster of gifts to this primary manifestation, my calling to visionary leadership becomes even more pronounced. My gift cluster includes faith, leadership, and teaching/preaching. Knowing how I am put together has kept me from taking "promotions" (callings?) to assignments that might have interesting but which would have limited my impact and sense of fulfillment because they would not have used all of my gifts. Those assignments would have put me in places of maintaining existing programs. Without a potential growth, adventures into new territory, or intellectually stimulating and faith-challenging problems, I would be bored.

STEP 4

What is your holy discontent? What moves you in your inner person? What challenge or need in our world do you feel compelled to address? What impact of sin and brokenness makes you sick in your stomach or even angry? If you could invest your resources in only one activity for restoration, what would it be? Your answer to these questions might give a suggestion of where you might be called to invest in the Restoration Project. You may be surprised at how your gifting and life experiences are situated for you to respond well to that holy discontent.

My holy discontent is to connect people to their true identity (Rescue) and life assignment (Restoration Project). I am always moved to do this with the backdrop of the nations in mind. When I am part of community mobilization to change our world for the glory of Christ, I soar. This holy discontent is quite obvious in the outflow of this book.

STEP 5

Stop and Pray. Give yourself plenty of time to engage this step. Take time to listen as well. Part of the discernment process begins with the belief that God has not changed and that he is still a communicating God. He might not speak to you orally. Then again, he might! He has multiple ways of communicating his message: a clear sense in your heart, a word or image flashing in your mind, a pronounced Scripture that keeps getting declared in or over your life, the word of another, an angelic visitation.

I find it helpful, in these moments of listening, to journal. When I write things down I might receive a confirmation at a later time that will give me confidence that I have indeed heard from the Lord. If I just record these impressions in my memory, I can easily second-guess the confirmation or even wonder if I had manipulated the situation or the information. I journal daily and thus this is a natural space of listening for me.

STEP 6

Recall what prophetic words or words of knowledge have been spoken over you in your life. How do these words line up with each of the reflection foci above?

I will give an example from my own life. I have been engaged in vocational ministry for over thirty years. This has led to many different applications of my gifting and strengths. I have always enjoyed one of these particular applications of my gifts: writing smaller pieces. Eventually I began developing files of potential books I felt were important for me to write, ones arising from my life experiences. For five years, though, a PhD dissertation took priority over those envisioned books.

Then, three years ago, I was at a conference where the speaker did not know me. After he spoke, he initiated a ministry time of praying and speaking over the people gathered, inviting people to approach the front of the auditorium if they wanted prayer ministry. He then left the platform and walked straight to me. The Lord had given him a word—he saw books coming out of me. He did not know this was a latent desire of mine.

In the three months following his declaration of this word, I completed my dissertation, and within six months I had defended it. Within six months after that, my first book was written. I have completed another since that time. I am completing this present book and plan on completing two more over the next six months. Just yesterday, in conversation with one of my life peer mentors, he suggested a book that I should write on a yet untreated topic. Something was unlocked in me in that prophetic word three years ago.

STEP 7

Take a 30,000-foot perspective on each of the stages of reflection. Is there a synthesis of theme or fresh insight from the flow of several components of your life? Is there a clear sense of what your calling is for this stage of your life? I emphasize stage as my calling has shifted in application due to a number of factors in life, some of which might seem banal (an accident, financial need, family stage, listening to leaders) and others which were quite spiritual (a prophetic word from someone who did not really know me, mysterious scriptural directives over a period of time, questions written in a journal that had direct answers by the end of the day).

This is where it is important to bring in the faith community for confirmation. Calling is always personal, but it is never individualistic. What you discover in this time of reflection take to your trusted accountability partners in faith. Share with them what you have discovered and see if you hear from them a response of affirmation. God will give your faith community the collective mind of Christ in those moments of seeking His face.

All of my callings or assignments came to me; I have not sought them out. God would move the ground underneath my feet, so my spiritual antennas would be up. In each case, there was strong affirmation in the body of Christ that the assignment was from God for me.

STEP 8

Once you have centered in on your calling, what steps do you need to take to be more proactive in fulfilling that calling? Think developmentally: What will you need to do to live more fully in your primary calling? Consider what changes you need to make in your stewardship of time and resources. Reflect on potential people in your sphere of influence who might be good partners in this calling. Rally a prayer support group to invite God's fruitfulness in the use of that call. Invite trusted people to mentor and coach you, those who are a bit further along in the journey but who are in a similar place of life investment. Then make some clear decisions and changes to invest in primary calling.

In Step 6 above, I mentioned the prophetic word that was spoken over me about the writing of books. That word unleashed something in the spiritual realm. However, there were some action steps that were needed for me to act on that calling. Simply put, I needed to cooperate with the spoken word by disciplining my extra time to write. Because I have a full schedule as pastor and adjunct professor, I have found the best time for creative writing for me occurs on vacations and on my days off.

Some people might wonder how writing fits into Sabbath rest on my day off. For me, it feels like Sabbath, as I get to use a creative side of my brain that is not always engaged in the day-to-day delivery of ministry and leadership. So my wife and I like to leave the house on a day off and find a coffee shop where I can write for three to four hours; afterwards, we move on to other restorative activities later in the day. We have also designed some vacation days during the slower summer season, and choosing days that surround my Sabbath days so I can enjoy a three-day block of time. We are blessed to have places that friends allow us to use, which have spaces of nature that enliven my soul and inspire creativity. I also discipline myself to write every morning on our longer vacations away.

My point is meant to be direct. Most callings will never have all the time and resources needed. We often need to make choices to focus our lives toward those callings.

So get at it! God wants you engaged in the Restoration Project. And you will be most alive when you are in that proactive partnership with Him.

Experiences – Passions – Gifting – Holy Disconnect - Calli

Life Achievements: List three key
moments at each stage where you felt
success.

Ages 0-12:
1)

2)

3)

Ages 12-22:
1)

2)

3)

Ages 22-now:
1)

2)

3)

Is there a pattern? Can you summarize
it in two to three words?

This is your MAP (Motivated Abilities Pattern). It
will keep seeping out in whatever you do.
Arthur Miller, The Power of Uniqueness

What have
personality
assessment
and after som

I am.....

Around others

What is your h
Hybel's notion
need in our wo
to address?

Stop and pray
has anything t
this moment.
minutes. Note

On the basis of the abo

Given this calling, I nee

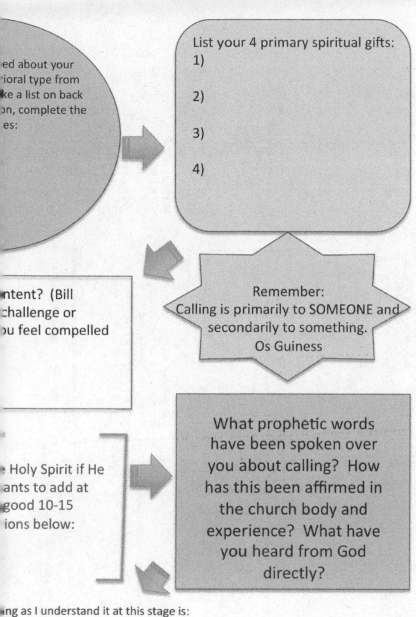

ed about your
...ioral type from
...ke a list on back
...on, complete the
...es:

List your 4 primary spiritual gifts:

1)

2)

3)

4)

...ntent? (Bill
...challenge or
...ou feel compelled

Remember:
Calling is primarily to SOMEONE and secondarily to something.
Os Guiness

...Holy Spirit if He
...ants to add at
...good 10-15
...ions below:

What prophetic words have been spoken over you about calling? How has this been affirmed in the church body and experience? What have you heard from God directly?

...ing as I understand it at this stage is:

...following to fulfill this call...

Experiences – Passions – Gifting – Holy Disconnect - Calling

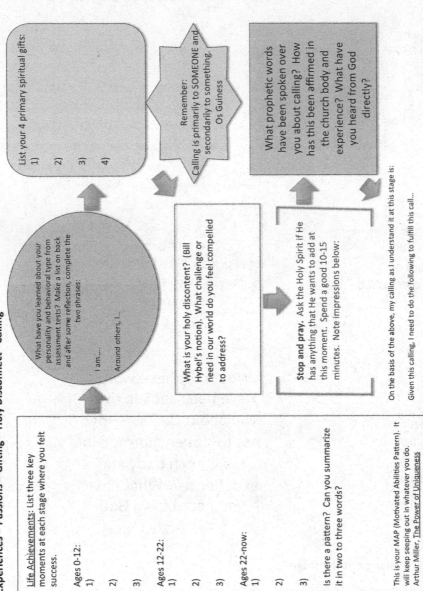

Life Achievements: List three key moments at each stage where you felt success.

Ages 0-12:
1)
2)
3)

Ages 12-22:
1)
2)
3)

Ages 22-now:
1)
2)
3)

Is there a pattern? Can you summarize it in two to three words?

This is your MAP (Motivated Abilities Pattern). It will keep seeping out in whatever you do. Arthur Miller, The Power of Uniqueness

What have you learned about your personality and behavioral type from assessment tests? Make a list on back and after some reflection, complete the two phrases:

I am......

Around others, I...

What is your holy discontent? (Bill Hybel's notion). What challenge or need in our world do you feel compelled to address?

Stop and pray. Ask the Holy Spirit if He has anything that He wants to add at this moment. Spend a good 10-15 minutes. Note impressions below:

List your 4 primary spiritual gifts:
1)
2)
3)
4)

Remember:
Calling is primarily to SOMEONE and secondarily to something.
Os Guiness

What prophetic words have been spoken over you about calling? How has this been affirmed in the church body and experience? What have you heard from God directly?

On the basis of the above, my calling as I understand it at this stage is:

Given this calling, I need to do the following to fulfill this call...

APPENDIX TWO

SCRIPTURE VALIDATIONS FROM GOD

"You were created exactly the way God wanted you to be" (Psalm 139:13).

"He has known you since the womb" (Jeremiah 1:5).

"You are fearfully and wonderfully made" (Psalm 139:14).

"He rejoices over you with gladness" (Zephaniah 3:17).

"He has ordained your times and places so that you would find him" (Acts 17:26-27).

"Nothing is lost in his plan. He has a way of assuming it all into your destiny" (Genesis 50:20).

"You were given a new identity in Christ when he rescued you" (II Corinthians 5:17).

"He calls you by name" (Isaiah 43:1).

"You do not need to make a name for yourself. He has given you a new name and it is so precious to him that he has engraved it on his hands" (Isaiah 49:16).

"He likes to remind you by his Holy Spirit how precious you are to him as his children" (I John 3:1).

"He whispers Abba Father to your heart" (Galatians 4:6).

"He bears witness to us that we are forgiven" (Hebrews 10:15-18).

"He reminds you that your adoption gives you full inheritance in his Kingdom family" (Romans 8:15).

"He stands as guarantee of your ongoing development into becoming fully like Christ" (Philippians 1:6).

"He will sanctify you wholly, body, soul, and spirit"
   (I Thessalonians 5:23-24).

"He has prepared works in advance for you to do" (Ephesians
   2:10).

"He wants your engaged will but it is his might that will bring
   the results" (Colossians 1:29).

"He has already positioned people around you and will be
   ordaining your movements so that others can experience his
   love" (I Peter 3:15).

"God does not lie, so you can count on it" (Titus 1:2).

ENDNOTES

CHAPTER THREE
1.   C. S. Lewis, *The Great Divorce* (New York: HarperCollins, 2000) n.p.

INTRODUCTION TO PART I
1.   Scot McKnight, *The Blue Parakeet* (Grand Rapids: Zondervan, 2008) 88.

CHAPTER FOUR
1.   Certainly other prophets deliver a message through prophetic action or symbol. Jeremiah visits the potter's atelier. Isaiah walked three years naked and barefoot. Ezekiel laid on his left and right sides for an extended period. Hosea married an unfaithful woman. But the majority of their messages came through oracle. Jonah speaks loudest through his actions and, more interestingly, actions contrary to the calling and manner of God.

CHAPTER FIVE

1. C. S. Lewis, *The Problem of Pain* (New York: Macmillan, 1962) 93.

CHAPTER SIX

1. John Ortberg, *The Me I Want to Be: Becoming God's Best Version of You* (Grand Rapids: Zondervan, 2010) 164.

CHAPTER SEVEN

1. T. A. Perry, *The Honeymoon Is Over: Jonah's Argument with God* (Peabody: Hendrickson Publishers, 2006) 52.
2. John Ortberg, *The Me I Want to Be: Becoming God's Best Version of You* (Grand Rapids: Zondervan, 2010) 237.
3. Thomas Carlisle, *You! Jonah!* (Grand Rapids:Eerdmans, 1968) n.p.

INTRODUCTION TO PART II

1. Alfred Corn, *Incarnation* (London: Viking Penguin, 1990) 310-311.

CHAPTER NINE

1. One interesting aspect of the biblical story is how chosen-ness gets marked through ritual and often through a new name. Abram becomes Abraham. Jacob becomes Israel. When Moses is called by God to re-unite that sense of chosen-ness to the slave-family, God marks the occasion by revealing to Moses a new name for himself: Yahweh. Simon becomes Peter, the rock. Saul becomes Paul. This renaming is interesting in light of the original struggle that is repeated through the chapters of Genesis—will the people give up making a name for themselves and allow God to give them a name. Chosen-ness is a bold process of identity establishment.

CHAPTER TWELVE

1 Ruth A. Tucker, *Guardians of the Great Commission: The Story of Women in Modern Missions* (n.p.: Academie Books).

CHAPTER THIRTEEN

1. Os Guinness, *The Call: Finding and Fulfilling the Central Purpose of Your Life* (Nashville: Thomas Nelson, 2003) 3.
2. Os Guinness, *The Call: Finding and Fulfilling the Central Purpose of Your Life* (Nashville: Thomas Nelson, 2003) 4.
3. Original source unknown. I first heard this definition of worship quoted by Ravi Zacharias in a Worship and Evangelism Class at Alliance Theological Seminary in the early 1980s. It has shaped my practice every day since.
4. Bill Hybels, *Holy Discontent: Fueling the Fire that Ignites Personal Vision* (Grand Rapids: Zondervan, 2007) n.p.
5. John Eldridge, *Desire: The Journey We Must Take to Find the Life God Offers* (Nashville: Thomas Nelson, 2000) 3.
6. J. Robert Clinton, *Leadership Emergence Theory* (Altadena, California: Barnabas Resources, 1989) 381.
7. Eugene Peterson, *Under the Unpredictable Plant: An Exploration in Vocational Holiness* (Grand Rapids: Eerdmans, 1992) 6.

CHAPTER SIXTEEN

1. Bill Hybels, *Holy Discontent: Fueling the Fire that Ignites Personal Vision* (Grand Rapids: Zondervan, 2007).

CHAPTER NINETEEN

1. Oswald Chambers, *My Utmost for His Highest,* Chaplain's edition (n.p.: Discovery House Publishers, 2005) Daily devotion for September 29.

CHAPTER TWENTY

1. Ravi Zacharias, *The Grand Weaver: How God Shapes Us through the Events in Our Lives* (Grand Rapids: Zondervan, 2010) 58.
2. Ruth A. Tucker, *From Jerusalem to Irian Jaya: A Biographical History of Christian Missions* (Grand Rapids: Zondervan. 2004) 460.
3. David Livingstone and Frank Garlock. "Lord, Send Me Anywhere," in *Rejoice Hymns.* n.p.

CHAPTER TWENTY-TWO

1.   Chuck Davis, *The Bold Christian: Using Your God Give Spiritual Authority as a Believer* (New York: Beaufort Books, 2013) 59.

CHAPTER TWENTY-FOUR

1.   Chuck Davis, *The Bold Christian: Using Your God Give Spiritual Authority as a Believer* (New York: Beaufort Books, 2013).

CHAPTER TWENTY-FIVE

1.   Timothy Keller, *King's Cross: The Story of the World in the Life of Jesus* (n.p.: Penguin Group, 2011) n.p.

CHAPTER TWENTY-SIX

1.   John Piper, *Let the Nations Be Glad! The Supremacy of God in Missions* (Grand Rapids: Baker Academic, 2010) 35.

CHAPTER TWENTY-NINE

1.   G. K. Chesterton, *Orthodoxy*. (n.p.: SnowBall Classics Publishing, 2015) n.p.
1.   Richard Stearns, *The Hole in Our Gospel: What Does God Expect of Us?* (Nashville: Thomas Nelson, 2014) 2.
1.   J. R. R. Tolkien, "The Last Stage," *The Hobbit* (n.p.).
1.   C. S. Lewis, *Yours, Jack* (New York: HarperCollins, 2008) 233.

APPENDIX ONE

1.   Arthur F. Miller, Jr. and Bill Hendricks, *The Power of Uniqueness: How to Become Who You Really Are* (Grand Rapids: Zondervan, 1999).